ordinary genius

also by kim addonizio

poetry

Lucifer at the Starlite

What Is This Thing Called Love

Tell Me

Jimmy & Rita

The Philosopher's Club

fiction

My Dreams Out in the Street

Little Beauties

In the Box Called Pleasure (stories)

non-fiction

The Poet's Companion: A Guide to the Pleasures of Writing Poetry (with Dorianne Laux)

anthology

Dorothy Parker's Elbow: Tattoos on Writers, Writers on Tattoos (coedited with Cheryl Dumesnil)

word/music cd

Swearing, Smoking, Drinking, & Kissing (with Susan Browne)

ordinary genius

a guide for the poet within

kim addonizio

w. w. norton & company new york • london

Printed in the United States of America
First Edition

For information about permission to reproduce selections from this book, write to Permissions, W. W. Norton & Company, Inc., 500 Fifth Avenue, New York, NY 10110

For information about special discounts for bulk purchases, please contact W. W. Norton Special Sales at specialsales@wwnorton.com or 800-233-4830

Manufacturing by LSC Harrisonburg
Book design by Chris Welch
Production manager: Devon Zahn

Library of Congress Cataloging-in-Publication Data

Addonizio, Kim, date.
Ordinary genius : a guide for the poet within / Kim Addonizio. — 1st ed.
p. cm.
Includes bibliographical references.
ISBN 978-0-393-33416-6 (pbk.)
1. Poetry—Authorship. I. Title.
PN1042.A348 2009
808.1—dc22

2008036211

W. W. Norton & Company, Inc., 500 Fifth Avenue, New York, N.Y. 10110
www.wwnorton.com

W. W. Norton & Company Ltd., 15 Carlisle Street, London W1D 3BS

10

for my students

contents

II. inner and outer worlds

III. the poem's progress

IV. toward mastery

acknowledgments

I would like to thank my editor, Carol Houck Smith, for her careful attention and valuable suggestions. Thanks to Margaret Gorenstein for her work on permissions; to my agent, Rob McQuilkin, for his enthusiasm and support; and to my students past and present, for sharing their love of the word and their imaginative lives.

introduction

This is a book about creativity. Poetry happens to be its main subject, because poetry is my main vehicle: my way of traveling through life, of taking in the world and trying to give something back. It is a book meant to inspire you, whoever you are, no matter your level of skill or ability, your age, or what circumstances brought you to these pages. It contains ideas about life and art, self-destruction and self-expression, difficulty and pain and failure, joy and ease and perfect moments. These ideas are meant to encourage you, challenge you, and lead you more deeply into your own life and poetic practice. It doesn't matter if you want to write only for yourself, or for publication. Whether you believe that you are wildly talented, or are haunted by the thought that you just aren't, and never will be, good enough.

Inspire: to breathe in.

Breathe in this book. You'll find ideas for making poems—a lot of them. Not every idea here is going to work for everyone, but there are some that will turn you sideways, jolt you into something completely unexpected, and keep you up nights. Some of the exercises are also aimed at leading you toward experiencing poetry in all its forms, rather than toward poems as end products. Poems aren't products, anyway. Poems are what you make when you experience life in a certain way. Alive to yourself in the world, observant of inner and outer reality, and connected to language.

A few years ago, I wrote a book called *The Poet's Companion* with another poet, Dorianne Laux. We wanted it to be a guide for people beginning to write poetry, an introduction to the pleasures of putting words together in surprising and beautiful ways. *The Poet's Companion* has been widely used in creative writing classrooms, and by many individuals starting out. It has also been helpful to poets already writing and publishing, because the exercises in it are just as fruitful for those with more skill and experience. Accomplished writers are always interested in new approaches to craft and new challenges to their imaginations. We all sometimes need a jump start, or a fresh perspective.

This book, like *The Poet's Companion*, contains discussions of the techniques of poetry as well as the process of creating it. Since publishing *The Poet's Companion*, I've continued to think about what good poetry is and how to encourage and guide my students in their own efforts. And since that book came out, the Internet has become an incredible resource for poets at every level, so you'll find many opportunities here to go back and forth between the online world and the book you're reading. You may, in fact, be reading this book online, or have downloaded it. In other words, this book is wide open to the discoveries you'll make reading poems, whether you find them on the printed page or in cyberspace.

Most of the exercises here are those I've invented since *The Poet's Companion*, for myself and my students, from teaching in settings ranging from juvenile hall to universities to my living room. There are a few I know I borrowed, and I apologize, but by now I'm not sure where they came from. All I know is that they have sparked new poems and directions for many writers, including myself.

I've also covered a few details regarding my own life and poetic process. I've never been particularly interested in writing a memoir. There is a lot of personal material in my poems already. Not all of it is literally true—poets, as you know or will soon discover, are good inventors—but if you've read any of my books, you will have some sense of who I am. This is the case for every poet and writer, even if we think we are composing complete fiction. Everything we write reveals us to others; that's just how it is, part of the contract. It has always helped me to hear how other writers have found their way. So I hope that reading about my creative life will help you to enter yours more fully.

"The purpose of art is to stop time," Bob Dylan said. That is what stories and poems do, what all art does. Art is energy, held in a form long enough to be experienced. A fresco on a church wall in Italy. A dancer's controlled movements, the drawing of a bow across a vibrating string. Or an exquisite arrangement of sticks held together by ice that will melt—until there is only a pile of sticks, a memory of the sculpture.

Poetry is an often misunderstood art. People think it's easy to write. They don't realize that it is as difficult to make a great poem as it is to make a great painting or blast out a virtuoso electric guitar solo. To understand poetry as an art is to understand that it is the same as every art, every discipline. It is work. Work that you struggle with and sometimes turn from in frustration or even despair. But also beautiful work you can go to in times of stress and loss. "Happy work," writer Anne Lamott calls it, "as gratifying as sex or hard laughter or love or good drugs."

There is a Latin saying: *Ars longa, vita brevis.* Art is long, life is short. But the true and beautiful thing is that nothing lasts. Everything changes and passes. The creative process is just that. Not a means to an end, but a continuing engagement with being alive.

Breathe in, and begin.

I.

entering poetry

✳ 1

leaping in the dark

There are so many ways to begin writing that you may feel overwhelmed by the sheer number of choices. You may have fears as well: fear of failure, of not writing well enough, of making yourself vulnerable to those who read your words. Many seasoned writers have felt the terror of the blank page, and have spent difficult periods, sometimes lasting for years, during which they simply could not begin the work they longed to do.

There is a lot of uncertainty in any creative act. Some people love this—it's what draws them, over and over, to make something out of nothing. Other people can't seem to get past it; they don't want to confront the unknown. It's useful to recognize that uncertainty is going to be there, however you feel about it. It's likely you will never reach the point at which uncertainty falls away completely. Former Poet Laureate

Stanley Kunitz, when he was well into his nineties, said it was as hard to write a poem as it had always been. He had read and written and studied for a lifetime, but he still had to go through this mysterious process of "not knowing" each time he sat down to write.

Agnes de Mille, the dancer and choreographer, said this: "Living is a form of not being sure, not knowing what next or how. The moment you know how, you begin to die a little. The artist never entirely knows. We guess. We may be wrong, but we take leap after leap in the dark." Every artist, in every field, will tell you something similar.

So given that you don't know where you are going, how do you take the first step?

The first step is this: Stop. By this I mean, Sit still for a moment. It doesn't need to be a long moment; a few deep breaths, enough to clear your head and center yourself in your body. The point is simply to experience your own awareness, without your thoughts chasing after the past or future. I've found that most of the time I take shallow breaths, unless I really focus on breathing differently. As soon as I begin to deepen my breath, I feel more connected to myself.

When you do this, you should be in a place where you are ready to write. It doesn't matter whether it's a crowded café, a desk, a kitchen table, or in bed with your laptop (which happens to be my favorite place; I once read that the French novelist Colette took to her bed the last ten years of her life, entertaining while propped up on pillows, and I felt a flash of envy and yearning). Give yourself half an hour in a place where you can write, and have some poems at hand for company and inspiration. If you have more time, great. But half an hour is all you need. It's possible to find that much time, even during a very busy day. Not having time may seem like the truth, but it's usually an excuse. Whatever the demands on your time—and for most of us, there are many demands beyond the making of poems—there is space somewhere in your day, or night, to set aside half an hour on a fairly regular basis.

This is important. Why? Because it's discipline. Because without a regular time, you are not committing yourself to what you say you want to do. If you really want to write—and this is a *big* if—you must make a commitment to that desire. Does this mean that you can't just play around and enjoy writing when you feel like it? Of course not. But if you want to see what poetry is really about, to unlock its secrets and gifts—and if you want to do it well—you must commit.

Years ago, I wanted to be a musician. I studied classical voice at American University in Washington, D.C., when I was twenty, and I was a miserable failure at it. I had never heard any classical music, let alone opera. I grew up in a suburban, sports-dominated household. Football and baseball, TV sitcoms and game shows: those were my cultural influences as a child. Also the books I discovered at the library, that took me to a different world, away from my family. At college I was shy and scared, and some of my music teachers were openly frustrated with me; some were unkind. I dropped out of college and eventually gave up wanting to become a singer. Next I took up the flute, and practiced seriously—three hours every day. I hoped to return to school in San Francisco, where I was now living, to finish a music degree. By now I was in my mid-twenties. I was working as a fry cook and waitress at a tourist restaurant, and figured I wasn't going to make a living as a musician. Maybe I could work with music and children in some way. Then I started writing poems, and I soon began to feel conflicting tugs at my energies. Look at it this way: I fell in love with poetry, and suddenly I didn't want to date the flute, or any other instrument, anymore. I knew that if I wanted to be any good, I had to focus.

As it turned out, music came back into my life later. In my mid-forties, I returned to my first love—not playing the flute this time, but learning blues harmonica. The focus on writing, from my twenties to my forties, had been crucial. Now I have to juggle the writing and the music, because I want to become a decent player. I can't give music what

I give my main job, which is writing, but I commit some time to my harp nearly every day.

So begin to focus yourself. Set aside half an hour three or four times a week—more if you can. Schedule it if you have to. Choose your spot, take those deep breaths, and honor your commitment to write.

⁂ 2

make a book

A book is usually considered the end result of years of study and writing and hard work—and it is exactly that. But the book I want you to make is more of a journal—one that will function as your creative space for the next week or month or semester. (I suggest a minimum of one month.) The book is a physical place to explore your imagination and experiences. Find one with blank, unlined pages. I feel that unlined pages allow for more sprawl; there's less of a sense that you have to follow rules. Spend some time making the outside of the book yours—with photos, collages, drawings, or whatever attracts you. Leave the first page of your journal blank. When it's finished, you can go back and title it according to what has ended up inside it.

Into your journal, put entries as often as possible. Copy poems you read, that speak to you in some way. On a facing page, note what those poems make you think about, or how they tug at you emotionally, or draw a picture or take a photograph that feels like a response. Add movie ticket stubs, pressed flowers, to-do lists, postcards, quotations, overheard conversations, anything and everything that has meaning for your life. You can write poetry in your book, of course. If you always work on a computer, print out drafts or finished poems and tape or glue them in. Think of your journal as a place with no boundaries or censors—it's pure, raw expression. The journal is the inside of your head as you travel through a certain amount of time. Later you can mine it, if you want; you can go back and pull out interesting lines and images and memories, find poems to revise and ideas to develop. That's one function of your journal.

The other function of your journal is to show you to yourself.

Leap, and the net will appear.

—*Zen saying*

3

first thought, worst thought

Beat poet Allen Ginsberg famously said, "First thought, best thought." He took it from an earlier poet, engraver, and visionary, William Blake: "First thought is best in art, second in other matters." The trouble is that when you sit down to write, your first thought isn't necessarily as wonderful as you'd wish. If your mind is very clear, maybe you will speak spontaneous brilliant poetry, like Rumi, the great thirteenth-century Sufi poet and mystic. But my mind is often full of junk—what I call "received thoughts." Ad slogans and TV commercial jingles. Sayings like "Life is a journey" and "You get what you pay for," and repetitive thoughts about my fears and desires and writing projects and plans for the weekend. The first thoughts that come to my mind are invariably banal, clichéd, or boring—all adjectives that would never be applied to good poetry.

What constitutes good poetry? Editors, critics, and readers all have their standards, and sometimes those standards differ. But just as you can tell a good singer from someone who can't carry a tune, you can, with a bit of practice, evaluate a poem. In writing, whether it's your first poem or your thousandth, the first language you get down on the page may not be the best, but it will give you material you can make into something stronger. The word "poetry," after all, comes from *poesis*, Greek for "making."

Here are a few of the qualities I respond to as a reader and try to achieve as a poet; they can guide you as you write, and as you work with a rough draft.

Surprise. A poem may use unusual words, but it often simply uses everyday words in surprising combinations, so that we see the world a bit differently. In "The Fish," Marianne Moore describes a mussel shell that opens and closes "like an injured fan." A good poem moves in surprising ways, taking us to places we didn't expect, avoiding the predictable.

Music. Imagined in the reader's head, or spoken aloud, words combine to move quickly or slowly, to screech or murmur, creating a rhythm that is married to the meaning. When Robinson Jeffers, in "Hurt Hawks," writes, "The broken pillar of the wing jags from the clotted shoulder," the choice and combination of words describes the injured hawk and how the writer perceives this bird's majesty (the wing is a "broken pillar"). Listen to the sounds as you read that line aloud. Notice the verb "jags," how we actually snag on that hard *g* after the sound of "the broken pillar of the wing." The adjective "clotted," paired with "shoulder," gives us two words that have the same rhythm: CLOT-ted, SHOUL-der, with the *l* in "shoulder" echoing the one in "clotted," and both of them echo the *l*'s in "pillar." It's a very musical line.

Detail. The Jeffers line, above, is an example of strong detail. Details convince; they persuade us that the writer has looked closely at the world, and they bring us close to the world the writer is creating. "Instant oatmeal with raisins and brown sugar" better describes my breakfast than "what I ate when I got up." When poems want to describe the physical world, they do so with specific detail. The writer evokes any or all of the five senses for the reader's imagination. If I describe my breakfast by saying, "The gluey oatmeal, the sweet raisins plumping up under the pour of hot water," I have just worked with the details to make them a bit more interesting.

Sufficient thought. Everyone knows that poems cover emotional territory. But of course they also involve the brain; they show the writer's mind. You may begin a poem in intuition, and revise intuitively as well, but at some point the logical part of your brain has to be invited to the party to help you achieve a poem that really explores and develops your subject. It may take several passes at a piece of writing to get there.

Syntax. Syntax is sentence structure. A good poet is a "language master," someone who knows not only about words but also about phrases, clauses, sentences, semicolons, periods. Samuel Taylor Coleridge said that a well-placed period can be like a spike to the heart. Most of us have gaps in our knowledge of sentence structure or grammar. The confusion between "lie" and "lay," for example, is widespread. Whatever your skills are in this area, they will develop the more you read and write.

The parts contribute to the whole. The "whole" often isn't very clear until you've spent some time working with the parts. Anything that doesn't add to the whole ends up taking away from it. If you are writing a poem about a divorce, that interesting description of your cat probably isn't adding anything. Could it? Yes, if it leads us back in some way to the divorce. Unity, coherence, focus on a theme—these are powerful tools for making a passionate piece of writing that will have a strong impact on a reader.

Mystery. William Carlos Williams called a poem "a machine made of words." In many ways that's a good definition, and tells us that he took craft very seriously. I like to think of a poem as a machine that has come to life; it has a pulse, one you can't find on any blueprint. When Sylvia Plath wrote, "Poetry is the blood-jet. There is no stopping it," she was talking about that pulse.

None of this is accomplished without effort. These elements don't magically appear in anyone's early work, but you can still invite them in, early and often. Novelist Kurt Vonnegut said that being a writer allowed him to edit himself into someone resembling an intelligent person. That's a nice way to think about moving on from your initial inspiration; you're going to make it better, more intelligent, as you go.

Some people get stuck in early drafts and find it hard to accept that they need to do more. Fear is often a factor here. If you produce a lousy draft, you may conclude that you are a lousy writer. Not so.

Dare to feel like a beginner—unsure and clumsy at first, but having a good time and doing your best to learn.

A couple of years ago, I took up trapeze. Every week, a part of me wanted to quit. I dreaded climbing the narrow ladder to a tiny platform thirty feet in the air—think of a doghouse in the sky, without walls. I felt that trapeze had no practical value—what was I going to be, the world's oldest aerialist?—and that I should be doing something else, like writing. My instructor was not particularly friendly or encouraging. When I landed in the net facedown (in ropes and a harness, to reduce the danger of instant quadriplegia), he gave me a look as I flipped off the side of the net. "I said *pull* on the bar, not *push*," he said. "You are supposed to *jump* from the platform, not *fall* from it." Fortunately he was also handsome, and French, or I might have quit right away.

But the thing is that I loved it, too. Once I was there, my mind was completely focused. There was too much energy running through me, too much concentration on whatever trick I was learning, to allow anything else into my head. It was complete presence, and that is addicting. Trapeze was beautiful for its own sake, whether or not I ever performed for anyone besides my instructor and the other students. It was skill and grace and daring, and it was thrilling.

If a poem came into my head at the moment I was flying, I might trust that it was good.

And the truth is that "First thought, best thought" is a great statement, taken the right way. It's about letting go of the conditioned mind—all of those received thoughts—and tuning in to some level of thinking that's deeper than our usual concerns. If you pay attention, you'll find that there are some weird and interesting thoughts floating around in your head. Very rarely, you may sit down to write and a poem will emerge almost completely formed, having arrived on the kind of inspiration we associate with genius. If this happens, it will be because you have worked hard preparing for the poem. You've faced your fear and climbed the ladder, and you've practiced.

4

getting started

Here are some exercises to get you writing. Language leads to more language. You can use these ideas when you feel blocked and need to reconnect with your muse, or, if you are new to poetry, as a way to begin. As with all the exercises in this book, you can change, adapt, or add to them as you see fit. The accompanying poems will give you examples and spark new ideas.

Often, I'll refer you to other poems. Most of them are readily available online. I usually just Google the name of the poet and poem I'm looking for. Often I'll print out a poem so I can think about it and reread it, and I'll paste it into my journal. You might want to do the same, and build a personal anthology of favorites. You can also seek out poems in libraries and the poetry sections of bookstores. If you like a particular poem by an author, you're sure to discover more work you'll enjoy when you pick up the book.

american sentences

It's easier to start with the goal of writing one short sentence than an entire poem. What interests me is how a short sentence can have all the qualities of a poem—a quick, perfectly executed brushstroke that surprises and delights, that's full of mystery and meaning, and set to a rhythm that sings. Allen Ginsberg, inspired by the traditional Japanese *haiku*—three lines of five, seven, and five syllables—invented the "American Sentence," one sentence of seventeen syllables. Here is his observation of a New York street scene:

> Four skinheads stand in the streetlight rain chatting under
> an umbrella.

Google "Ginsberg" and "American Sentences" to read more. Or see his 1994 book *Cosmopolitan Greetings*. There is also a web site at www.americansentences.com.

Here are some American Sentences written by my students:

> Spooky dream of mom in the shower saying *I'm a black*
> *ambulance.*
>
> —*Andy Crockett*

> Marylou walks around her block with a greyhound
> and a cigarette.
>
> —*Amy Hoffmann*

My boyfriend's stereo equipment creeps across our living room floor.

—Kathleen Boyle

This world and all the creatures in it are on fire and some of you know it.

—Nion McEvoy

Once you pulled a towel over my head and told me all your secrets.

—Lauren Peck

My brother has five thousand books, so why do I wrap these up for him?

—Ellen Perry

What's key here is the moment sharply observed, a brief "aha!" of pleasure or recognition or awareness. Begin with whatever is in your immediate environment, and then expand into memory, into ideas, to see what comes up. After that, change your work space. Get up and look out the window, or take a walk and jot down notes about what you see. Then revise your American Sentences so that they sound both specific and musical. You can do this exercise every time you begin to write. It's a good warm-up, like playing musical scales.

Sometimes, you can reorganize sentences from the many you've written, combine them, and end up with an interesting poem.

You'll find more concrete ways to use your sentences as springboards for poems in the next chapter, "Opening Doors." If you're new to poetry, you may want to read that chapter, and the following one about the line, to gain some confidence with your first poems. Or you can simply start writing, keeping in mind some of the qualities of a good poem listed in the previous chapter.

start with a line from someone else

The first lines of poems often let you know a bit about the world you're entering. They can tell you who is speaking, indicate the subject matter of the poem and tone of voice, set up a rhythm, present a situation. First lines can be highly abstract, or drop the reader into a specific scene.

Read through this list of first lines and think about what each one sets up. Choose one and let it lead you into your own writing—a paragraph or two of prose. Or, you could try lines that are of about the same length as these.

- A sudden blow: the great wings beating still
- Bent double, like old beggars under sacks,
- Beyond all this, the wish to be alone:
- Come sleep, Oh sleep, the certain knot of peace,
- Come to me in the silence of the night;
- Downhill I came, hungry, and yet not starved;
- Groping back to bed after a piss
- Half of my life has gone, and I have let
- How do I love thee? Let me count the ways.
- If there exists a hell—the case is clear—
- I hold my honey and I store my bread
- I sought a theme and sought for it in vain,
- No longer mourn for me when I am dead
- Obscurely yet most surely called to praise,
- Remember me when I am gone away,
- Something there is that doesn't love a wall,
- Sundays too my father got up early
- The house was quiet and the world was calm.
- Thou ill-formed offspring of my feeble brain,

All of the above lines are iambic pentameter: roughly ten syllables, five da-DUMs that create a lilt you can hear. There will be further exercises later to fine-tune your ear. If you've already experimented with this meter, you can try turning what you've started into *blank verse*, unrhymed iambic pentameter.

Now read some of the poems in their entirety. Many can be found online, and all of them are in *The Norton Anthology of Poetry*, Fifth Edition. See how each first line introduces the rest of the poem. Here is a well-known poem about World War I from Wilfred Owen:

DULCE ET DECORUM EST

Bent double, like old beggars under sacks,
Knock-kneed, coughing like hags, we cursed through sludge,
Till on the haunting flares we turned our backs
And towards our distant rest began to trudge.
Men marched asleep. Many had lost their boots
But limped on, blood-shod. All went lame; all blind;
Drunk with fatigue; deaf even to the hoots
Of tired, outstripped Five-Nines that dropped behind.

Gas! GAS! Quick, boys!—An ecstasy of fumbling,
Fitting the clumsy helmets just in time;
But someone still was yelling out and stumbling
And flound'ring like a man in fire or lime . . .
Dim, through the misty panes and thick green light,
As under a green sea, I saw him drowning.

In all my dreams, before my helpless sight,
He plunges at me, guttering, choking, drowning.

If in some smothering dreams you too could pace
Behind the wagon that we flung him in,
And watch the white eyes writhing in his face,
His hanging face, like a devil's sick of sin;
If you could hear, at every jolt, the blood
Come gargling from the froth-corrupted lungs,
Obscene as cancer, bitter as the cud
Of vile, incurable sores on innocent tongues,—
My friend, you would not tell with such high zest
To children ardent for some desperate glory,
The old Lie: Dulce et decorum est
Pro patria mori.

Owen drops us vividly and immediately into a terrible scene, a battle that haunts the speaker. The title and last line derive from the Roman poet Horace: "It is sweet and decorous to die for one's country." Given the evidence here, Owen tells us that dying for one's country is anything but sweet and decorous. The title reveals itself as ironic. Owen's opening portrays the reality of combat on the ground, rather than from the lofty distance of noble ideals. The physical details—the men "trudging," "blood-shod," fumbling with their helmets, the dying man "choking," blood "gargling" from his mouth—are a powerful argument for Horace's statement about "the old Lie."

After reading the poems with their opening lines, you may be inspired to go back to your initial writing and revise it, tightening or adding, working with the sounds, honing it for greater detail and clarity.

More exercises:

1. Take a first line you like and rewrite it in your own words, based on your experience. For example, "Sundays too my father got up early" might transform into "Every Friday, he brought home

KFC." "Come to me in the silence of the night" might become, "Come over, when my parents are asleep." Start a poem based on your line.

2. Take a line from someone else and change one word in the line: "Beyond all this, the wish to be alone" might become, "Beyond all this, the wish to be perfect." See where you can go from there.
3. Look in the dictionary to find different nouns and adjectives beginning with the same letter as the words in someone else's line. "A sudden blow, the great wings beating still" could become, "A sick bell, the guttural whisper banging sadly." You may need to go through a few substitutions before you hit on one that excites you and feels like a starting point.
4. Take a line from another writer and use it as the *last* line in your poem. This is what Wilfred Owen did, borrowing that line from Horace. And here is William Matthews's "Poem Ending with a Line From Dante":

E detto l'ho perché doler ti debbia
—Inferno, xxiv, 151

Snow coming in parallel to the street,
a cab spinning its tires (a rising whine
like a domestic argument, and then
the words get said that never get forgot),

slush and backed-up runoff waters at each
corner, clogged buses smelling of wet wool . . .
acrid anger of the homeless swells
like wet rice. This slop is where I live, bitch,

a sogged panhandler shrieks to whom it may
concern. But none of us slows down for scorn;

there's someone's misery in all we earn.
But like a burr in a dog's coat his rage

has borrowed legs. We bring it home. It lives
like kin among the angers of the house,
and leaves the same sharp zinc taste in the mouth:
And I have told you this to make you grieve.

Matthews's poem starts with an epigraph: a quotation from Dante's *Inferno,* the first book in Dante's masterful thirteenth-century trilogy, *The Divine Comedy.* The epigraph is translated into English in the final line. The poem opens with a vivid, melancholy scene: the snow, the futile spinning tires of the cab that suggests the residue of a bitter quarrel. Everything is soggy with hopelessness. The anger of the panhandler infects the speaker, who passes it on to the reader, so we in turn "bring it home." If this were your poem, what would you describe to make us grieve? Or see the famous ending of James Wright's poem "Lying In a Hammock at William Duffy's Farm in Pine Island, Minnesota," a quiet meditation that suddenly lifts off with its last line, "I have wasted my life." How would you prepare a reader for that statement?

start with a title

Titles draw us in even before first lines. They can be simple and not give away too much: "Bird," "Night Song." Or they can deliver a lot of information, as in the James Wright title above. A title is a first impression that may be confirmed and deepened by the poem itself. Or the poem may turn the title on its head, surprising us. Or it may do both: Wright's poem does, indeed, take place on a farm in Minnesota, as the speaker lies in a hammock. But the suggestion of ease—what could be more relaxing than a hammock on a farm in a small Midwestern town?—is gradually undermined by the feeling of loneliness in the poem, and is finally and suddenly taken away by that unexpected last line.

Below are the titles of several poems. If you read the entire poems, you'll understand more about how the titles function. The following exercises will give you a way to begin working with your own titles.

1. Write a long title which, like these, gives a lot of specific information. Then expand on it in your own poem:

   "Tell Me Again How the White Heron Rises Across the Nacreous River at Twilight Towards the Distant Islands," Hayden Carruth
   "Hard Rock Returns to Prison from the Hospital for the Criminal Insane," Etheridge Knight

2. Write a poem for the end of something, with "last" in its title. For example:

   "Last Poem," Ted Berrigan
   "Last Call," me and probably a lot of other writers
   "Last Trip to the Island," Erin Belieu
   "The Last Time I Saw Richard," a great song by Joni Mitchell

3. Name a specific time and/or place in your title, and then write a poem about that time, that place. It might involve a series of events, a particular event, or a single moment of observation. Read these first:

   "Memories of West Street and Lepke," Robert Lowell
   "Massacre, October '66," Wole Soyinka
   "Composed Upon Westminster Bridge, September 3, 1802," William Wordsworth

"Easter, 1916," William Butler Yeats

4. Title your poem "On Turning ——," and fill in your latest birthday, or a memorable one. The convention is to mourn one's lost youth when reaching middle age or old age. For a comic turn on this, read "On Turning Ten" by Billy Collins.

5. Write a poem using any of the titles below. I invented these, except for the first one, which an instructor assigned in my first creative writing class my senior year of college.

   "My Life in the Circus"
   "Life on Earth: A Report to the Emperor of a Distant Galaxy on the Habits of Humans"
   "Why Animals Mate"
   "In Praise of Failure"
   "God in the Details"
   "The Most Beautiful Thing in the World"
   "My President"
   "Losers in Love"
   "The Sadness Factory"
   "The World According to My Cat [Dog/Parakeet/Snake/Goldfish, etc.]"

start in the middle

The first example in the "borrowed lines" exercise above opens "Leda and the Swan" by William Butler Yeats: "A sudden blow, the great wings beating still." The poem begins *in media res*, in the middle of things. As in "Dulce et Decorum Est," there is tension, or trouble, immediately, a sure way to grab the reader's attention. In that exercise, there are a couple of examples of people who can't sleep. I was probably drawn to these because I wake up somewhere between 4 and 5 A.M. nearly every night. The middle of the night, I've found, can be a good time to write; there are still fragments of dreams I can remember, and I don't feel like there's anything else I have to do, so I pull my notebook over (often it's in my bed already) and jot down whatever occurs to me.

Write ten openings that begin *in media res.* Think about setting up trouble and expectation. After you've written them, study them or show them to someone else—a writing partner, your writers' group, a class—and see if you can make them more specific and/or create more tension. Choose the three you like best, and free-write on each one for five minutes without stopping.

If you're in a class or writing group, pass your sentences to someone else to use, and use theirs. Do three more timed five-minute writings on these sentences.

Another way of starting in the middle: Write something that you want in your poem, that you know is not the opening. It might be a bit of research you did, a note you made to yourself—even some language you are sure isn't going to end up in the finished poem. Do it anyway, as a place to begin. The idea is just to take one little area of the piece and fill it in: a description, a moment, even a single line. Anne Lamott, in *Bird by Bird*, calls this the "one-inch window." For example, you know you want to write about a rainstorm, but you don't know how to start; it sounds dumb to begin, "It's raining." You know you want to talk about not only the rain that's falling right now, but how it stormed during your father's funeral; you remember the awful repetition of the windshield wipers going back and forth as you sat in the back seat of the car. So put that down. Begin with that image from the past, though you think the poem will eventually begin with the present. Now you've moved from staring at the blank page to getting down some language. You've started. Later you can figure out how to put the parts together.

start from memory

Write about someone you remember from high school. Keep yourself out of it except as an observer of that person's experience. (Read Thom Gunn, "The Butcher's Son.")

Write about a first experience. (Read Elizabeth Bishop, "First Death in Nova Scotia"; Philip Levine, "Gin.")

Write about where you were and what you were doing when you got the news of a major world event.

Write down three powerful emotional memories—one of happiness, one of grief, and one of love. Write three poems, or combine the three memories into one poem.

Write about something you wish you could remember more clearly, and try to imagine what you can't recall.

write to the future

Read these, then write your own version of a poem to the future. You might address all human beings, or a particular one, like a child coming into the world, or your own future self.

"To Those Born Later," Bertolt Brecht
"People of the Future," Ted Berrigan
"Look to the Future," Ruth Stone
"A Phone Call to the Future," Mary Jo Salter

love potion number 9: start from the next thing you see

In the pop song "Love Potion Number 9," the guy who's "a flop with chicks" takes a drink and starts kissing everything in sight. An earlier version is the tale of Tristan and Isolde. Tristan is a knight escorting Isolde by ship to her future husband, King Marke, in Cornwall. Before they get there, they unwittingly drink a love potion, and fall in love.

So look up from this book, and fall in love with the first thing or person you see. Your latte, the café worker, a bottle of ketchup, a bird out the window, a panel truck passing. Whatever. Write about it, talk to it, focus on it rapturously.

A variation: Jot down a list of things you see around you and fall recklessly in love with all of them.

start from language

Here's an early creative writing exercise I was given: Choose fifty favorite words, and write a poem using those words. My poem began, "The Uzbek floozy burbled on the hurdy-gurdy," and ended, "oh, oh, the olallaberries." Make your list and then write from it. You might also exchange word lists with someone else.

Now try mixing in a list of your favorite words with words from some other source—a cookbook, a textbook, a billboard ad. Then use those words as a springboard to more writing.

Another way to start from language: Skim through a book of poetry and select random words that interest you, then use them to write.

Here's a possible variation on the above:

1. Choose a contemporary poem, or two, that you really like.
2. Make a list of all the nouns in the poem(s).
3. Make a list of all the verbs.
4. Make a list of all the adjectives.
5. Choose six nouns, five verbs, and three adjectives.
6. Use five of the nouns, all five verbs, and the three adjectives to create a poem of your own (you'll probably want to add some words).
7. The sixth noun is the title of your poem.
8. The first sentence or line of your poem should exactly copy the rhythms, but not the language, of the first sentence or line of one of the poems you drew your words from in the first place.

In your journal, keep a list of new words you learn. (You'll find my list later in this book.) Keeping a list will also clue you in to whether you are, in fact, learning many—or any—new words. My mother was always reading books with titles like *Build Your Vocabulary.* So as a child I picked up odd words, like *peripatetic* and *xanthus,* from her. The *Word A Day* calendar is a good tool; each day you can learn the word and try to write a poem that includes it. Simply writing down the words and their definitions will help fix them in your memory; using them in poems will make them yours.

My mother also looked up words in the dictionary and told us their Greek and Latin origins. For a while it drove me crazy. I would say something like, "I think I'm going to throw up," after eating too much Halloween candy, and she would say, "Regurgitate. From the Latin *re,* meaning again, and *gurgitare,* to engulf, flood. It probably has the same root as *gorge.*"

Look up a word's roots, and write a poem that explores or includes that information. Here's a lyrical prose poem by A. Van Jordan that immediately mixes in the speaker's own associations and memories. In a prose poem, there are no line breaks, but the other elements of poetry can all come into play. Jordan manages to have it both ways: though his piece is written as a block of prose, it creates rhythms not only through the language, but through those slashes that makes us pause as though we're reading lines.

> **af ter glow** n. 1. The light esp. in the Ohio sky after sunset: as in the look of the mother-of-pearl air during the morning's afterglow. 2. The glow continuing after the disappearance of a flame, as of a match or a lover, and sometimes regarded as a type of phosphorescent ghost: This balm, this bath of light / This cocktail of lust and sorrow, / This rumor of faithless love on a neighbor's lips, / This Monday morning, this Friday night, / this pendulum of my heart, / This salve for my soul, / This tremble from your body / This breast aflame, this bed ablaze / Where you rub oil on my feet, / Where we spoon and, before sunrise, turn away / And I dream, eyes open, /swimming / In this room's pitch-dark landscape.

Ntozake Shange used slashes in the same way in her powerful play, *for colored girls who have considered suicide / when the rainbow is enuf.* Shange called her play, made up of poems about being African-American and female, a "choreopoem." In the West African tradition, the poet, or *griot,* sings and tells the stories of the tribe. Whether you're exploring the roots of a word or the roots of your own tribe or family, there is a wealth of material to draw on. Fill up on language; gorge on it, then give it back as nourishment: new poems, better than Halloween candy.

5

opening doors

Imagine a sentence as a hall with a series of doors. Each door is a possible way to use what you've already written to generate new material. Once you have an opening sentence (one you've borrowed from another writer, say, or an American Sentence of your own), you can open those doors and discover ways to go further.

Essentially, a door is a part of the sentence you can use as the basis for a repetition. Repetition and pattern make a poem both musical and memorable. If you're stuck in a piece of writing, or feeling uninspired, you can use this technique not only to intensify the music, but also to move into new language and surprising territory.

Here are some sentences and possible doors.

First Door: Repeating Several Words

I read her my poems and she said, "Oh, I am so sorry for you!"
—American Sentence by Nion McEvoy

I read her my poems and she said, "Oh, I am so sorry for you!"
I read her the newspaper and she said, "Oh, I am so sorry for
everyone else."
I read her a novel and she said, "Oh, I'm so sorry, I don't like
novels unless they have happy endings."
I read her my old love letters and she said, "Oh, I am still so sorry
for you."

By building on Nion's opening sentence, I've painted a portrait of a relationship. Here's a different spin on the same sentence; this time I've repeated several words, but changed the idea:

I read her my poems and she said, "Oh, I am so sorry for you!"
I read the newspaper and it said the world was a sorry place.
The menu said, "Sorry, there is nothing here to satisfy your
hunger."
And the billboard told me I was a sorry loser without a luxury car.

These two American Sentences by Amy Hoffman create an interesting pair because of repetition:

Today I found a twenty in the red-lined pocket of my wool coat.
There's no twenty-dollar bill in the red lining of my uterus.

Second Door: Repeating the Opening

Anaphora is the repetition of an opening word or phrase, like "I read" in the first example above. Anaphora is a powerful tool, used by Walt

Whitman, Allen Ginsberg, and legions of other poets. Look how it can work, building on a borrowed line from Robert Browning's "Andrea del Sarto" to exploit the word "but" and the concept of argument:

But do not let us quarrel anymore,
but on the other hand it's all your fault,
but I understand you didn't mean to do it,
but in fact you did, you lousy prick.
But I forgive you. Really, it's no problem,
but I can't let it go, it's so unfair,
but fine, okay, whatever: I forgive you.
But why should I forgive you? You still did it.

(There's another door here besides the word "but." I've repeated the rhythm in each line, too.)

Third Door: Repeating the Ending

In the tradition of Alaskan Inuit poetry, the last word or phrase of a line gets picked up in the beginning of the next. So the lines might go something like:

I went down to the river,
the river that flowed east,
east toward the sun.

Here are two lines from a Kiowa song, from Jerome Rothenburg's *Shaking the Pumpkin: Traditional Poetry of the Indian North Americas:*

I don't care if you're married, I'll still get you,
I'll get you yet.

So here's my extension of the first line of Sonnet 71 by Shakespeare:

No longer mourn for me while I am dead.
Death is no big thing.
The thing is, I won't know if my friends,
my friends who are alive, I mean,
I mean I might have some dead friends by then, too,
by then you might not be around to mourn me.
Me, I'm alive right now, so why are we,
why are we being so morbid?

Fourth Door: End Rhyme

Rhyming is another way to generate a new direction. Suppose you wanted to take off from the opening of "To Sir Toby" by Philip Freneau:

If there exists a hell—the case is clear—

Usually, when I'm looking for an end rhyme (a rhyme at the end of a line), I'll list several words, to see if they spark an idea. *Clear-near. Clear-door. Clear-there.* A rhyme doesn't have to be exact. In fact, it's often more interesting when it isn't. Rhymes are echoes, so any sound that echoes another can be considered a kind of rhyme. Sometimes the echo is strong, as in *clear-near*, but it can also be less obvious: *clear-ignore.* So, I might jot down a few more rhymes for *clear: dear, where, here, core, fear, jeer, peer, before, blear, stare.* I'll include words that seem dumb or unlikely: *beer* (hmm, maybe after all that would be a good one), *seer, steer*, etc.

Now it's time to fool around, and see if anything gets interesting:

If there exists a hell—the case is clear—
It's probably not below us, it's right here.

or:

> If there exists a hell—the case is clear—
> You'll find it after too much beer.

or:

> If there exists a hell—the case is clear—
> There's no heaven anywhere.

Here's an American Sentence by Andy Crockett:

> Nutmeg latte, Elton John, car window part way down—
> portable world.

Some possible end rhymes: *cold, fold, curled, hurled, pearled, sealed, old, chord, bored, told, healed.*

A possible start on a poem, then

> Nutmeg latte, Elton John, car window part way down
> —portable world.
> I wish I could stay like this forever, never arriving, sealed
> into this music, these nostalgic chords that make me feel young.

In the third line, the word *chords* has become, not end rhyme, but internal rhyme—a rhyme within the line. The sounds are stitched together, but less obviously. Internal rhyme is another way to open a door.

Fifth Door: Syntax

Syntax—sentence structure—is a crucial part of any writer's craft. There are many ways to explore syntax, and I'll be talking about more of them later. For now, just notice what you can do if you pay attention to the way the sentence is set up. This opening is from "The Owl" by Edward Thomas:

> Downhill I came, hungry, and yet not starved;

This line contains an inversion of normal word order, not something you usually want to do unless you want to sound like you were born in the nineteenth century, like Thomas. Today, you'd probably write, "I came downhill." After the subject and verb there's an adjective, "hungry," the contraction "yet," signaling opposition, the negative "not," and another adjective, "starved"—more extreme than "hungry."

So, suppose you want to figure out a new line and use the door of syntax. We're going to leave the opening phrase alone, and play with repeating the second part, "hungry, and yet not starved":

> Downhill I came, hungry, and yet not starved;
> depressed, and yet not bipolar,
> drunk, and not yet alcoholic,
> lonely, and yet not isolated . . .

Here's another example. It's a lot like Mad Libs, that party game in which the parts of speech are taken out of a paragraph and left blank, to be filled in by those who haven't seen the paragraph. Substituting new words that serve the same function in the sentence leads to surprise, and often humor.

This opening line is from William Butler Yeats's sonnet "Leda and the Swan":

> A sudden blow: the great wings beating still
> (article, adjective, noun, article, adjective, noun, verb, adverb)

Playing with the possibilities, you might produce:

The unbearable truth: an enormous beast descending forever

or:

A quickening fire: a sickening weight bearing down

Clearly you'd need to vary this strategy pretty quickly, but it's enough to get you started—and to give you a feel for good syntax from the inside.

Here's another quick take on expansion through syntax:

But do not let us quarrel anymore.
And never let us speak again.
Or always let us try forever.

Sixth Door: Expanding the Sentence

Write an opening sentence. Now delete the period, add a comma, and then add one of the following words or phrases to your sentence:

but	although
or	because
and	when
like	in spite of
as if	etc.
as though	

Here's an American Sentence by Kathleen Boyle:

A new apartment, a chance to wipe it all clean, to begin again.

A possible expansion:

A new apartment, a chance to wipe it all clean, to begin again
as though I'd never lost anyone, or myself, like a newborn,
or the first creature made from mud, or clay . . .

Once you begin to see the doors in sentences, and in parts of sentences, you can use them not only to create new poems, but also to gain a deeper understanding of poetry. Here's the beginning of a poem by Robert Duncan; you can see how he's opened some of the doors I've described:

OFTEN I AM PERMITTED TO RETURN TO A MEADOW

as if it were a scene made-up by the mind,
that is not mine, but is a made place,

that is mine, it is so near to the heart,
an eternal pasture folded in all thought
so that there is a hall therein

that is a made place,
created by light
wherefrom the shadows that are forms fall.

Look at how the repetitions hold the poem's music: "that is not mine" is followed by "that is mine"; "made place" is said twice, for emphasis. "Heart" and "thought" and "light" echo each other, as do "hall" and "fall." The phrase "near to the heart" is paralleled by "folded in all thought." The image of the "eternal pasture" is extended with "so." Duncan probably didn't create such music in his initial draft. It's likely he opened some doors the first time around, and then went back to look for more.

✳ 6

your genius, your demons

If I lose my demons, I will lose my angels as well.

—*Rainer Maria Rilke*

When I was younger, much as I longed to be an undiscovered genius who would one day uncover the one thing I was naturally brilliant at, I knew I was not brilliant. In high school I loved English class and reading books, but I never thought seriously of becoming a writer. When I started college at Georgetown University, my writing wasn't considered good enough for acceptance to honors English. In fact I didn't know what I was doing at Georgetown. In theology class, our professor drew an apple and an onion on the board. The point was: What if life is an onion and not an apple—what if you peel away the layers and there is nothing at the center, no core? I think that's how I felt then—like an onion. I dropped out of Georgetown after three weeks. Two years later I returned to college, to American University, where I lasted two and a half years before washing out as a classical voice major. I finally earned my bachelor's degree when I was twenty-eight, at San Francisco State, and it wasn't until that final year that I fell in love with poetry after reading Sylvia Plath. I enrolled in Introduction to Creative Writing to learn about this powerful, mysterious art form. The following year, certain that I wanted to become a poet, I started in the master's program.

Before wanting to be a poet I did many things: worked hateful low-paying jobs, lived in a lot of group houses, took up the flute, read, drank, took drugs, found my way in and out of friendships and love relationships. My life didn't change once I discovered poetry. But I had found my direction. I didn't have a great aptitude—my early poems were truly terrible—but I had a calling at last. I realized that poetry was my gift. My "genius."

According to Roman mythology, the *genii* were gods who watched over particular people and places. Each man had a genius, a spirit who had given him being, who taught him and protected him. Each woman was said to have a *juno.* So maybe I should say that I found my juno. It didn't matter that I didn't know how to write poems yet. I had discovered the thing that I wanted to keep close to me for the rest of my life, and if I did that, my tutelary spirit would watch over me, would teach me what I needed to know.

This is your genius: your own profound desire to write. Your love of words and language, your attempt to get to what poet Donald Hall called "the unsayable said." If you are meant to be a writer, you will serve your genius as well as you can. If not, you'll find your genius elsewhere. You may still love to write, but it won't be the main thing you serve. Forget wondering, *Am I good enough? Can I do this?* The only thing you really need to ask yourself is: *Is writing my genius?* If it is, then apprentice yourself.

When I started to write poetry, I had no idea how to begin to learn about it. I don't even remember how I came across that fragment of Plath. I would walk into bookstores, find the poetry section (usually hidden in a corner of the store), and buy books whose covers I liked. One of the first books I bought this way was Denise Levertov's *Life in the Forest.* The cover showed a black-and-white image of a transparent woman among the trees. I had other teachers in graduate school, but books and poems were my first teachers, and they continue to be the best. Though I always longed for a mentor—that one person who would take me in hand and teach me exactly what I needed to know—I never found that person. All this time—twenty-some years—I have had to rely on my genius.

I've already said that you need to commit to your desire to write. For many people, not getting to the work becomes the first demon. One definition of demon is this: a persistently tormenting person, force, or passion. But if you look into the origins of the word, you'll see that it comes from *daemon,* from the Latin for "spirit," which derives from the Greek *daimon,* "divine power." Which, of course, leads us full circle to this: an attendant spirit; a genius.

Your demons are there to be used and overcome, and in this sense, they are ultimately helpful. Did you think writing great, or even good, poems would be easy? What feeling of accomplishment would you get from doing what is easy, what anyone can do without trying? Athletes train relentlessly to become stronger, faster, better. Dancers attend class every day, and rehearse long hours in the studio. Actors memorize thousands of words and then practice saying them over and over, working to inhabit their characters. If you thought poetry was different, this is your wake-up call. Poetry is a bitch. It wants your energy, your intelligence, your spirit, your time. No wonder you want to avoid it. I know I sometimes do. But the only way past, as I read somewhere, is through. Put your ass in the chair (or the bed), and get started.

Once you do that, other demons will show up.

There are the demons of self-doubt and belittlement. Mine currently sound something like this: *Lately I feel like I've been writing the same poem over and over. Maybe it's because I haven't read enough. I should never have talked my way out of that required course in the nineteenth-*

century novel in grad school. I should be more political. No, wait, I think I should really be more personal. But somehow universal, and not narcissistic. How do I do that? I don't know. I need to find some other direction. What is it? Something is missing, and I don't know what it is. To hell with it, I give up.

My journals are full of the word *can't* when it comes to my writing. Another word that appears often is *nada*, "nothing." *Nada, nada, nada* shows up over and over in my journals. But even *nada* is writing. Somewhere in the next few pages after *can't*, and *nada*, there's a scrawled mess of words and arrows that means I'm trying to work out a poem.

Many artists have struggled with lack of self-worth, with feelings of insufficiency. But this didn't stop them from creating. It may, in some cases, have propelled them into creation. Art is a way of dealing with hopelessness, with anger and despair and loss. It is a creative response. While there is a real distinction between art and therapy, the truth is that art is therapeutic. It helps you to take something that is within you and make a place for it outside of yourself.

This doesn't mean that you don't also create art out of joy. Even the blues has a lot of joy in it. There's a long tradition of ecstatic poetry: Kabir and Rumi and Hafiz, Mirabai and Saint Teresa of Ávila and Hildegard of Bingen. William Blake wrote *Songs of Innocence* as well as *Songs of Experience*. In every culture, there are poems that celebrate God or the gods or the Great Spirit, the body, love and desire, the earth, the harvest, pleasures great and small. The Psalms of the Old Testament are praise songs. The Bible contains beautiful poetry about God's wisdom and mercy, along with his righteous wrath and punishment. Your demons and your genius are never far apart.

Maybe some of your demons are these, or variations: Your uncle abused you. Your mother was cold and self-involved. Your beloved brother died, or your father. You never had a sister, though you wanted one. You grew up poor, envious of people with houses, with phones and electricity that never got cut off. Or you grew up comfortably middle-class, fairly happy, and now you feel you have nothing interesting to draw on for writing. Secretly you feel too boring or stupid to write good poetry. You felt ugly as a child; you still do. You don't know if you can truly love anyone. You are afraid to leave the house some days. You can't make small talk. Or you talk too much, and lie in bed in the middle of the night regretting things you said. You cut yourself in secret, or gorge on food, or drink too much.

Everyone has demons.

One of my students showed me a web site called PostSecret. You can find it at www.postsecret.blogspot.com. People write and illustrate their secrets on postcards, and mail them to this guy, and he puts them on his site. It's a fantastic project. There are four PostSecret books now. After looking at the web site, I was inspired to create some postcards of my own.

Make a postcard, or several, about your secrets. Put the postcards into your journal. You might want to send one to PostSecret.

Sri Aurobindo, an Indian yogi, poet, and political leader, said: "You carry in yourself all the obstacles necessary to make your realization perfect. Always you will see that within you the shadow and the light are equal. If you discover a very black hole, a thick shadow, be sure there is somewhere in you a great light. It is up to you to know how to use the one to realize the other."

new words

sequacious (si-KWAY-shuhs) adj. Unthinkingly following others.
hellkite (HEL-kyt) n. An extremely cruel person. [From the Middle English *hell* (a place of misery) + *kite* (a person who preys on others).]
thank-you-ma'am n. A bump or depression in a road. [From the nod of the head that results when one passes over it in a vehicle, as if in acknowledgment of a favor.]
verbigeration (vuhr-bij-uh-RAY-shun) n. Obsessive repetition of meaningless words and phrases.
titivate (TIT-i-vayt) v. tr., intr. To make smarter; to spruce up; to decorate.
pollex (POL-eks) n., pl. *pollices.* The thumb. [From the Latin.]
hallux is the big toe.
vomitorium (vom-i-TOR-ee-uhm) n. A passageway to the rows of seats in a theater. [From the Latin *vomitorium,* from *vomere* (to discharge).]
camorra (kuh-MOR-uh) n. A secret group united for unscrupulous purposes. [After Camorra, a secret organization in Naples, Italy, engaged in criminal activities, mostly during the nineteenth century. From the Italian, possibly from the Spanish (dispute).]
cockshut (KOK-shut) n. Evening; twilight. [Apparently from the time when poultry is shut in to rest.]

✳ 7

line, breath & vision

Not all poems are written in lines. The opposite of this is also true: Not everything written in lines is a poem.

> It's pretty clear
> that you can't just write a sentence,
> chop it into several lines,
> and call it a poem.

What I just wrote works as information, but falls flat as a poem. Why? Maybe because *it contains no poetry.*

Poetry isn't what we think of as the ordinary, but what we feel and sense is *underneath* the ordinary, or inside it, or passing through it. Poetry is the essence of the human spirit and imagination; it can be playful, irreverent, sarcastic, intellectual, despairing, filled with longing or anger or happiness. It can tackle the largest subjects, like Suffering and Love and Death and the Meaning of Life; and it can be about the smallest events: a beetle inching along a stick, shampooing a friend's hair, plums falling on the sidewalk. In fact, a poem is about both the ordinary and the extraordinary at the same time, because it recognizes that they are the same thing. William Blake wrote,

> To see a World in a Grain of Sand
> And a Heaven in a Wild Flower,
> Hold Infinity in the palm of your hand
> And Eternity in an hour.

This is clearly a different animal from the earlier four lines. "To see a World in a Grain of Sand"—that's a line to wake you up. A way of seeing *and* a way of saying. Read Blake's lines aloud and you'll hear their music: the rhythms of each line, and then the rhythms all together; the end rhymes of *Sand-hand* and *Flower-hour;* the sounds and rhythms of *Infinity-Eternity;* the two lines "To see . . ." and "Hold . . ." each followed by a line beginning with "And . . ." The "hour" at the end is both a measure of time and a concrete reference to something used to measure time (in the early nineteenth century, "hour" could mean "hourglass"). There's a sense of both meaning and something beyond it contained in a particular shape—a shape we can hear if we pay attention.

The line, in poetry, has been called a "unit of attention"; that's a good definition. A good poem will reward close attention, line by line.

In the beginning, you are likely to write a lot of bad poems. You will flounder around, unsure of what you're doing. You'll write lines that are perfectly clear to you that no one else understands. You'll write lines you feel are breathtaking in their beauty, only to have someone say, "That's a cliché. I've heard it a million times before." Don't worry about it. Read, and write, and read some more, and you will get better.

So given that you may be writing bad poetry at this point, or poetry that isn't yet quite what we mean by *poetry*—should you just forget about the line?

Of course not. The line is still important. Maybe your metaphors aren't brilliant yet, either, but you learn by doing (and by reading, which I will say often). So here are a few exercises to help you experiment with the line, in free verse; we'll get to the metrical line later.

lines and sentences

The paragraph below—you could call it poetry, since there is clearly poetry in it—is by Jean Toomer, an African-American writer, from his 1923 book *Cane*. A mix of verse, prose, and drama, *Cane* is considered to have kicked off the Harlem Renaissance.

BLOOD-BURNING MOON

Up from the skeleton stone walls, up from the rotting floor boards and the solid hand-hewn beams of oak of the pre-war cotton factory, dusk came. Up from the dusk the full moon came. Glowing like a fired pine-knot, it illuminated the great door and soft showered the Negro shanties aligned along the single street of factory town. The full moon in the great door was an omen. Negro women improvised songs against its spell.

Here are two ways this paragraph could be broken into lines:

version 1

Up from the skeleton stone walls,
up from the rotting floor boards

and the solid hand-hewn beams of oak
of the pre-war cotton factory,
dusk came.
Up from the dusk
the full moon came.
Glowing like a fired pine-knot,
it illuminated the great door
and soft showered the Negro shanties
aligned along the single street
of factory town.
The full moon in the great door
was an omen.
Negro women
improvised songs
against its spell.

What does this version accomplish? Well, the word "up" gets importance by being placed each time at the beginning of the line. It makes sense to emphasize "up," given that the poem talks about what is rising above the Negroes down in their shanties, or working in the factories for white bosses. The line breaks here are also working with the syntax of the sentences; that is, there is a line break where you might naturally pause, where there is a comma or a complete phrase or clause. A line break is a pause. (Denise Levertov felt it lasted "a half-comma.") Each moment gets a bit of attention before we move on to the next: we see the walls, and the floorboards, then the oak beams. The words "dusk came" are echoed by "the full moon came." The last three lines, though, don't seem to work so well. Maybe it's that each line has two beats (say them aloud and you'll hear them), and it feels a bit heavy to end the poem with a sound like stomping. For a softer ending, you might break the sentence this way:

Negro women improvised
songs against its spell.

Now you have two three-beat lines, instead of the reverse. And if that doesn't satisfy you—assuming this is your poem—you might rewrite, adding or dropping or changing words to create different lines.

Some poets like to begin with prose, while others write line by line as they find their way into their poem. The Toomer piece was written as prose and not meant to be broken up in this experimental way. But doing so can show you that even a good sentence may not make a good line.

version 2

Up from the skeleton
stone
walls, up
from the rotting
floor boards and the solid hand-hewn beams of oak of the pre-war cotton
factory, dusk
came. Up from the dusk the full
moon came. Glowing like a
fired pine-knot, it illuminated the great door and soft showered the
Negro shanties aligned along the single
street of factory
town. The full moon in
the great door was an omen. Negro women
improvised
songs against
its
spell.

This version has a certain jazzy energy, but I wouldn't say it knows what it's doing. The rhythms are jerky, an effect that doesn't fit the scene. We're pulled from single-word lines to very long ones without apparent reason. The whole piece feels as if it has gotten away from the writer. Compare the opening lines of this version with version 1. Version 1 sets up a regular rhythm; it emphasizes the syntax of the sentence with "Up, up"; and it also focuses on the words at the ends of the lines, the physical setting—walls and floorboards.

> Up from the skeleton stone walls,
> up from the rotting floor boards

Many poems, whether metered or free verse, establish a regular line like this throughout the poem. Others might be more irregular, but for a reason. The reason is usually a rhythmic one—how quickly or slowly the lines move, within how much silence—and/or a visual one: how the eye perceives the type against the white space (I think of the blank page as a kind of visual silence).

When you read and study poems, listen to the silence at the end of each line. Look at the white space surrounding the words. The writers of those poems didn't just slap words onto the page; they thought carefully about the effects of their lines. Try to get a feel for how different poets use lines. This will help you when you write your own poems.

As an exercise: Write a prose piece, then break it into lines. Look for a line length that seems to work for the prose, and try to make each line about that length. You may need to change, add, or delete words from the original piece to create lines of equal length.

Using the same subject, and without looking back at the first piece you wrote, write a new piece that you compose line by line.

Study the differences.

the rhythm and the meaning

Listen to this galloping line by Charles Bukowski:

The days run away like wild horses over the hills.

And this lilting, happy one by Dylan Thomas:

Now as I was young and easy under the apple boughs

And these bleak lines from Alfred, Lord Tennyson:

Break, break, break,
on thy cold gray stones, O sea!

And these from Gerard Manley Hopkins:

Generations have trod, have trod, have trod;
And all is seared with trade; bleared, smeared with toil;

And these from May Swenson:

I always felt like a bird blown through the world.
I never felt like a tree.

Notice how the rhythms in each of these examples fit with what the lines are saying. Can you hear the difference between a light line and a heavier one? A slow line and a faster one? Can you hear what certain sounds do—the feeling of *bough* and the feeling of *break*, or *trod, trod, trod, trade, bleared, smeared*? Tune your ear. Listen. Even the punctuation is important. Imagine the Hopkins example (from his poem "God's Grandeur") without it:

> Generations have trod have trod have trod
> and all is seared with trade bleared smeared with toil

Now write some lines of your own in which the rhythms echo the idea or mood you are going for. Try these, inspired by the above:

> A line about the passage of time
> A line about your childhood
> Two lines about the ocean
> Two lines about work
> Two lines: I always felt like a ——. / I never felt like a ——.

breath & vision

Charles Olson wrote an essay called "Projective Verse" in which he talks about the energy of a poem—from the energies that stirred the writer, to the "high-energy construct" of the poem, to the transfer of that energy to a reader. Once the poet moves away from a given form, where line length is determined (you'll understand this better when we get to meter), he or she is involved in "field composition." The poet is "out in the open," following perception rather than logic, attentive to the energies of the unfolding piece. The page is your field. It's a big, white, blank silence that, if you are writing free verse, you—and eventually your reader—will have to negotiate, line by line, moment by moment.

Some writers—and I am one of them—stick fairly close to the left-hand margin of the page. If you do that, you will come to hear what your line is doing, and you will always have the same unit of silence, of the same duration, to work with. Within your line you'll have the relative silence of a comma or semicolon or colon or period. Or you can create spaces between words and begin to move away from the margin:

> Up from the skeleton   stone walls,
>   up from the rotting floor boards   and the solid
> hand-hewn beams of oak   of the pre-war cotton factory,
>   dusk came.

As you move across the page, the white space comes into play. Any musician will tell you that silence is an important part of the music. Similarly, white space is part of the poem.

Scientists have discovered that outer space—what we think of as space—isn't. It turns out there is something they call dark matter, and it exists between the stars. So maybe for the poem, the page is white matter, rather than blank space.

If a word seems isolated when it is the only word in a flush-left line, imagine how forlorn it might be if stranded in the middle of a page. Consider how long it will take the reader to travel the distance to the next word or group of words. You might fragment words as well as sentences for interesting and meaningful effects. You could play with capital letters, italics, making words on the page larger or smaller. E. E. Cummings may be the most well known example of a writer using typography and white space, but there are others. Take a look at the poems of John Cage, the twentieth-century composer, writer, and visual artist; and of Michael McLure, a member of the Beat Generation. There's a difference between reading words that lead you to look at something beyond them, and words that make you look *at* them. You're more likely to look at a fragmented word. Is this useful or interesting? It depends on what you do with it.

One effective use of typography can be found in "Sabla Y Blu," a poem by singer-songwriter Tom Waits. Waits uses nonsense syllables to capture the feel of a trumpet solo by jazz great Dizzy Gillespie. Written mostly in capital letters, the poem reads like a loud, joyous improvisation. It opens,

SABLA Y BLU
SABLU BLAAA *BY* BLAA

—and ends with the words ASA Y BLU repeated several times, the line getting smaller each time, the sounds getting quieter, fading out on the last line:

ASA Y BLUE Y BLU Y BLU Y BLU Y BLU Y BLU Y BLU

Be aware that you can USE CAPITALS FOR EMPHASIS, *and italics, too,* but don't let that substitute for interesting language and thinking.

Take a poem you've written in conventional left-margin lines, and explode it onto the page. Try these techniques:

1. Keep the same line breaks as in your conventional version, but arrange the lines to make use of the entire page.
2. Words often contain other words, or can be disassembled in interesting ways. Look at what E. E. Cummings does in "spoke joe to jack," about an argument over a girl named alice:

   jack spoke to joe
   's left crashed
   pal dropped

   Simply by moving the possessive *'s*, Cummings conveys the sudden movement from a verbal argument to a physical fight. Try breaking apart some words for meaningful effect.
3. Take a breath, and read some prose you've written until that breath

naturally runs out. Let that determine your line length for the piece. How long a line is it? Arrange your "breath lines" on the field of the page.

4. Devise a system for arranging the words of your poem on the page. You might place abstract words five spaces in. Or put the word "I" in the middle of the page every time it appears. Words you want to emphasize could be in a column down the right-hand side of the page or oppositional words on opposite sides. See if you can dream up ways to make the arrangement of your language engage with its subject matter.
5. Another E. E. Cummings poem, about Buffalo Bill, opens with a few short lines about Buffalo Bill riding on his horse and then hits us with a rushing line followed by another that brings us up short:

> and break onetwothreefourfive pigeonsjustlikethat
>   Jesus

You can hear the breathless amazement in the speaker's voice, and then the pause of the white space, followed by the sudden exclamation of admiration: "Jesus."

Experiment with clumping some words and lines together, and separating others. For example:

You might write three lines
that begin
at the left margin,
                    then one in the middle of the page,
                                                  then drop down
                                                  for the next two.

Experience the differences when language is surrounded by other language, or by itself.

6. POETRY
   R
   E
   E

   This is a common exercise: Write a poem in the shape of the thing you are describing. Google these poems: "Easter Wings" by George Herbert; "Swan and Shadow" by John Hollander. Think about how the visual form of the poem relates to its content. A poem about a disastrous Christmas might become ironic if written in the shape of a Christmas tree.

7. Use the line break to create a surprise for the reader, a turn of thought, as in the opening of Sharon Olds's "The Promise." We are introduced to a couple sitting together at a restaurant, holding hands, presumably having a romantic evening, and then get these lines:

   > we are at it again, renewing our promise
   > to kill each other.

   The revelation of the nature of the promise dramatically reverses—or at least complicates—our expectations. Try something similar at the opening of a poem, and go on from there.

   You can also write a line that shifts our understanding more subtly. Here's the opening of Billy Collins's "The Literary Life":

   > I woke up this morning,
   > as the blues singers like to boast,

   What first seems a statement of unself-conscious fact, a simple "Here's what I did today," becomes, in the second line, very aware of itself as a poem, and as a kind of opening that is a part of a tradition of opening lines. (Singers from Robert Johnson to Jim Morrison have used "Woke up this morning" as a way to launch their songs.)

8. Write some poems that consist of very long lines. Get a feel for what seems to work in this particular form—for how quickly you need to release information, how the poem flows. Read poems by Walt Whitman, Robinson Jeffers, Allen Ginsberg, and C. K. Williams—all of them use the long line beautifully. When you've written something that seems to work pretty well, break the poem into very short lines.

   If the exercise is successful, you should feel that the short lines ruin the poem.

9. In the poems you've written so far, what kind of lines do you tend to write: regular or ragged, long or short or somewhere in between? At this stage—at every stage of your life as a writer—experiment. Get out of your comfort zone and try something different with your line breaks.

stop and go

You can take the reader on a relatively smooth journey, as in version 1 of "Blood-Burning Moon." The ends of lines offer little rest stops—a comma or period. Even if there's no punctuation, a line containing a complete thought or phrase creates a feeling of ease:

> up from the rotting floor boards
> and the solid hand-hewn beams of oak

The phrase has ended, and so has the line. The meaning of the line is completed, until we go on to the next one.

Version 2 is more like someone driving a stick shift who doesn't know how to work a clutch:

> street of factory
> town. The full moon in

The adjective "factory" is unmoored from its noun; the preposition "in" has no object until the next line. And there seems no reason for the poem to move in such a jerky fashion. By contrast, here is the opening of "Edge" by Sylvia Plath:

> The woman is perfected.
> Her dead
>
> Body wears the smile of accomplishment,

Now the adjective "dead," separated from the noun of "body," creates a sense of shock, emphasizing the body, the idea of death, and the mood of dread.

As for punctuation: A period is like a red light. If you put it at the end of your line, your reader will pause there longer than at a comma. I suppose a comma is a yellow light, as long as you're one of those drivers who slows down and doesn't step on the gas to beat the light. The dash, I think, fits somewhere in the yellow zone. Nothing at the end of the line, then, is a green light; your reader goes right on to the next line, though it takes a moment to cross the intersection and arrive there.

To continue the metaphor: Your line breaks—and your punctuation or lack of it at the ends of lines—control the flow of traffic.

The pace of your poem is also affected by what you do *inside* the line, as in the earlier example from Hopkins. "And all is seared with trade; bleared, smeared with toil." The line is heavy, defeated, and slow—a dirge of a line appropriate to the writer's vision of a sublime world ruined by the drudgery of work and commerce.

Select a poem by another writer, and map out for yourself what is going on with the line breaks. What's happening at the ends of lines? What kinds of rhythms are set up in each line? How do those things intersect with what the poem is saying? What patterns can you detect?

Once you've figured out at least some of what the poet is doing, try a poem of your own, borrowing those techniques. Copying has long been used by painters, so they can understand kinetically what the great artists were doing. It's also a useful way to learn about how poems move.

Here's the opening of a poem by C. D. Wright, "Nothing to Declare":

> When I lived here
> the zinnias were brilliant,
> spring passed in walks.
> One winter I wasn't so young.
> I rented a house with Anne Grey
> where she wrote a book and I could not.
> Cold as we were on the mountain
> we couldn't be moved to the plain.
> Afternoons with no sun
> a blanket is left on the line.
> Hearts go bad
> like something open on a shelf.

The pattern here is relatively short lines, about the same length, with several end stops. The first sentence takes up three lines, the next one, one. The next eight lines are four sentences of roughly equal length and similar rhythms, spread over two lines. Even noticing this much, you've got something to go on for your own piece.

Here are a few lines I wrote, inspired by Wright's poem. You'll notice

I've copied other things as well: the opening "When," a little of the syntax, a statement about love to go with Wright's statement about hearts.

When I loved you
the nights were neon
martini glasses edged in light.
Loneliness was drugged and locked in a room.
We never went in there
if we could help it.
Blind as we were
we always saw starlight.
Then the stars dimmed
and the blackness got brighter.
And love set sail
with no navigator.

My piece is a little too much like Wright's to make me comfortable calling it my own poem. The point of copying this closely is simply to get a feel for the lines and rhythms of a strong piece of writing. The artists who copied Rembrandt did so to learn about painting, not to be lesser versions of the master. They imitated as a way of looking closely, and then used what they had learned to develop their own work, brushstroke by brushstroke. Line by line, you can do the same.

✳ 8

by heart: a shakespeare sonnet

When you memorize a poem, you have it "by heart." This is a good way to know a poem. Even if you don't study it, you will understand it more just by knowing the words. You'll have a relationship with that poem. Once you memorize it, the poem will be yours.

Why start with Shakespeare? Why a sonnet? Here are some reasons:

1. He was really, really good at writing sonnets.
2. A sonnet is only fourteen lines. It also has meter and rhyme. Those things make it a snap to memorize, in comparison with a lot of other poems.
3. In memorizing, you'll also get a sense of the sonnet's structure. The traditional sonnet develops an argument, and that makes it easier to learn; you can do it in chunks.

4. You will impress everyone by being able to recite Shakespeare.
5. I mean, everyone.

If you're nervous about memorizing, you have a lot of company. In most of the schools and in some of the private classes I've taught, I've required my students to memorize a poem and recite it to the class. This exercise made them much more nervous than sharing their own poetry.

Later, they all thanked me for making them do it. I think they were sincere.

Here are some memorization tricks I know:

1. Choose a poem you want to learn or understand better, or one you flat-out love.
2. Give yourself a deadline: some social occasion or get-together with a friend or family, an open mic, anyplace you can announce that you've memorized a poem. Start working on it well ahead of time. If you save memorizing for the last minute, you'll blow it when you try to recite the poem.
3. Carry the poem with you—in a purse or backpack, folded in your pocket, or taped to the dashboard of your car. Put a copy of it in your journal. Try breaking it up on flash cards, a few lines on each card. Find a recording, if you can, to listen to. There are more and more poetry recordings and podcasts available online. You can find hundreds of free audio files at www.poets.org. Or you can record your own reading of the poem and listen to it. If you run, recite the poem to yourself while running. I memorized most of Keats's "Ode to a Nightingale" while jogging in Golden Gate Park. Make the poem your constant companion, so you know it cold. When the time comes to recite it, you won't forget it even though you're nervous.
4. Use the repetitions in the poem to help you remember. Those might be rhymes, rhythms, repeated words, repeated sounds in a line.

Here's the Shakespeare sonnet I'm about to memorize, number 73. I love its sad beauty, and I have always loved saying the line "Bare ruined choirs, where late the sweet birds sang" without quite remembering how the rest of it went.

> That time of year thou mayst in me behold,
> When yellow leaves, or none, or few, do hang
> Upon those boughs which shake against the cold,
> Bare ruined choirs, where late the sweet birds sang.
> In me thou see'st the twilight of such day
> As after sunset fadeth in the west;
> Which by and by black night doth take away,
> Death's second self, that seals up all in rest.
> In me thou see'st the glowing of such fire,
> That on the ashes of his youth doth lie,
> As the deathbed whereon it must expire,
> Consumed with that which it was nourished by.
> This thou perceiv'st, which makes thy love more strong,
> To love that well which thou must leave ere long.

This poem, a traditional English or Shakespearean sonnet, has fourteen lines and breaks easily into parts of four, four, four, and two lines. Each four-line section, or quatrain, has alternating rhymes, and also is self-contained. So when I memorize it, I'll probably take it one quatrain at a time. The *s* sounds in the line beginning with Death—"Death's second self, that seals up all in rest"—will help me remember that one. The "In me thou see'st the glowing of such fire" echoes "thou mayst in me behold" in the first line, and also "In me thou see'st the twilight," so I'll not only remember it, I'll feel just where those words come back. I'll also notice how the word "late" in "where late the sweet birds sang" leads to the idea of twilight. And after "black night" and Death, I'll think of "the glowing of such fire" as a star in the sky, and it will also remind me of those "yellow leaves" from earlier in the poem. There is also the underlying rhythm of the iambic pentameter: da-DUM da-DUM da-DUM da-DUM da-DUM—to keep me on track.

The process of learning a poem this way helps you pay attention. And it will help you to experience how a good poem unfolds in time, how its language feels in your mouth. When you finally recite the poem, say every word as if it were the name of someone you love, and you will deliver that energy and power to your listeners.

9

describe this

The great twentieth-century Russian poet Anna Akhmatova lived through the Russian Revolution and the Cold War. During her lifetime she endured the banning of her writing, the death of two of her three husbands—one was executed after their divorce, another died in a Siberian labor camp—and the years-long imprisonment of her son. Near the opening of her poem "Requiem," she writes of waiting in a long line with other women outside the prison. One woman turns to her and asks if the poet can describe the scene. "I can," Akhmatova says, and that "I can" sums up, for me, every poet's art and responsibility.

Description is important because it's evidence. One meaning of evidence is "outward sign." In a trial, physical objects may be entered as evidence, as proof. To follow through on "I can" is to say: *This happened.*

There is an Irish proverb: "The most beautiful music of all is the music of what happens."

And what is it that happens? Everything. Life is constant, unending creation and destruction, happening at every moment. There is always something going on. While you are reading these words, babies are being born, people are committing suicide or making love or torturing other people. Surgeons are leaning over anesthetized patients in modern hospitals, or operating without proper instruments in tin-roofed lean-tos. A big rig is fishtailing on a freeway in Oakland, a man is shaking open a newspaper in Pakistan, a woman is squeezing a cassava melon in an open market in Liberia. People are talking on cell phones, baking cookies, making copies, drilling holes in walls, sitting on buses, waiting in line, drinking beer and tea and frappuccinos, getting sick, hitting softballs, lying, taking pills, painting, throwing pots, dancing, falling, writing.

There are too many things happening to ever get to the end of describing them. As Chilean poet Pablo Neruda wrote in his beautiful "Arte Poética," there is "a swarm of objects that call without being answered." And not only objects but events, emotions, ideas.

It's amazing to me that all of this is happening at once, and yet I sometimes find myself wondering what there is to write about, and whether I have anything left to say. If you sometimes feel like this, it's good to go back to the evidence of the external world, to pay attention to the music of what happens. The world won't ever fail you. Even if you feel bored, if you think that nothing is happening, it only takes a little checking in with the evidence to prove you wrong.

I am often unaware of what is going on around me. When I lived with a photographer, he would often see things I didn't. "That woman at the restaurant," he would say, and I would answer, "What woman?" Because he had a keener visual sense, he had taken note of her, how she was missing a finger on her left hand, how she drank two martinis in a row, slugging them back, how her male companion kept looking at the woman at the next table. I often need to prod myself to really look at something, to get out of my internal world and register what is in front of me.

We register the world through our senses: what we see, hear, taste, touch, smell. The old creative writing cliché to "show, don't tell," is useful advice to the extent that most beginning writers are eager to talk about something before they bother describing the "something." The tendency is to skip the descriptive part, the evidence, and go straight to the idea.

For example: She is so beautiful.

For example: I am locked in the prison of my mind.

For example: The wealthy exploit the poor.

These statements lack the evidence to convince us, even if we may agree with what the writer says. The writer has the experience in memory, but hasn't yet passed it on to us. And we want the experience.

"Show, don't tell" is not ultimately so useful, though. Poets tell us things all the time. Abstract statements are in fact an important part of poetry. And what the poet chooses to *show* us, and how, is part of what the poet *tells* us. If you describe a house that "clings to the side of the cliff," you are doing more than showing us the house; you are also telling us something about how you see that house. This same house might "rise higher than the cliff" or "be visible for miles, like a beacon," or "squat forlornly with its fallen-in roof." It is hard, if not impossible, to describe things objectively. And objective description isn't the task of poets. We aren't surveyors, measuring the terrain and reporting numbers. We're looking for the essence of the land.

So the following exercises are meant to help you pay attention, to give you a point of departure.

stare

Staring is considered impolite, but go ahead. Maybe study is a better word to use. Study someone you don't know: a café worker or patron, a child playing on the sidewalk outside your window, your waiter or waitress or bartender, the post office clerk as you wait in line. Write down everything you notice about this person and what he or she is doing. This is a good exercise to do with a partner; both of you can choose the same person, and compare notes to see if one of you saw something the other didn't.

You can use this exercise in a number of ways. First, simply to get into the habit of truly seeing other people. If you live in a city, as I do, you may tend to let other people glide across your awareness. It's part of how we keep our personal space in cities. This exercise asks you to get close. First, by describing the person very specifically. Then you can take it further: Invent a life for this person, a reason she is wearing a red wool scarf and hoop earrings, a reason he is reading a medical textbook and jiggling his foot. Create this person's story, using the details at hand.

Noticing others will alert you to their individuality, their peculiarities. In my novels, when I want some minor character to become vivid in the reader's mind, I search for an unusual or precise detail. Remember the woman at the restaurant I just mentioned? You probably do, because of the missing finger, or the martinis. The odd detail can make a person, or a scene, vivid to a reader.

So besides getting into the habit of noticing people, pay attention to what is different about them. Keep a list:

> curly-headed boy wearing his T-shirt inside out
> homeless man on the sidewalk eating takeout with a metal fork
> woman with burn scar on the back of her neck

Use your observations to create characters for poems. Imagine them: what their lives are like, what their joys and sorrows are. Look beyond your own life.

common objects

Many books on creative writing suggest that you take a common object and study it, writing down everything that you notice, then connecting the object to an association, a memory, an idea. That's a good exercise; try it. B. H. Fairchild's "Cigarettes" is a terrific example.

This exercise is a little farther out; I got it from fiction writer Rebecca Brown. I'm re-creating it from memory, so it may be a bit different from Rebecca's exercise.

List several ordinary objects around you. You can do this anywhere. Right now, I can list these: towel, TV, dresser, vase of flowers, dropped shirt.

Next, choose two of those objects.

The first object is in love with the second object. Write about that love. Maybe the shirt is longing to be reunited with the dresser. Or the TV is wildly flipping channels for the entertainment of the flowers. Invest these ordinary objects with human feelings, and let your imagination create their world.

This is an excellent exercise to do if you are in love, or have just lost a love, or are obsessed with someone who does not love you, or are lonely for someone to love.

Another variation: Study an object closely, and think about its inner life. Does an object have an inner life? A friend once asked me, "Does the chair have a soul?" For your purposes, consider that it does. Maybe it resents not being a table. After all, a table gets to have food placed on it, and elbows, and candles. You know what a chair gets. So choose your object, and don't forget the physical description as well as the emotional.

one photograph

When Rebecca Brown and I taught together in the low-residency M.F.A. program at Goddard College, she took one, and only one, photograph, each day for the twelve days of the residency. Try this yourself for, say, five days.

Now, using the five photographs, describe what is in them and why you took them. Even if you don't know why, speculate.

Write about a photograph you would have liked to have taken, but didn't. Describe the picture that is in your head.

challenge the evidence

We conceal so much about ourselves. Like not really looking at other people, this is a necessary survival mechanism. But since poetry is about inner reality as well as outer reality, try this:

Choose a photograph of yourself, or of someone you know: parent, friend, sibling. Describe the external things the photograph shows, and the reality it seems to portray. Then describe why, and how, the photograph is a lie.

the muse in museum

I love looking at art for inspiration. I don't know a lot about how visual art works, but I feel its effects on my writing. I like having an experience with something that doesn't involve words, but is still the product of an artist's vision.

Ekphrasis is the term for writing about a work of art. Ekphrasis was popular with the English Romantic poets in the early nineteenth century.

"Ode on a Grecian Urn" by John Keats is a famous example. The poem closes with these lines: " 'Beauty is truth, truth beauty,'—that is all / Ye know on earth, and all ye need to know." It's an ambiguous statement: Is the urn telling us that beauty is everything, or is the poet telling the urn that all *it* needs to know is beauty, that humans need the experience of life? The poem is full of questions and paradoxes. Keats describes the various figures on the urn, fixed in unchanging scenes. A group of young men chasing after their "maidens" will never catch them; but the young women won't ever "fade" or grow old. The scenes—and the urn—last longer than our human life. The poem lasts, too. Keats didn't make it to old age; he died at twenty-six, not knowing that his own art would last. He composed his own epitaph for his tombstone, which reads, in part, "Here lies One Whose name was writ in Water."

Here's the poem:

Thou still unravished bride of quietness,
Thou foster child of silence and slow time,
Sylvan historian, who canst thus express
A flowery tale more sweetly than our rhyme:
What leaf-fringed legend haunts about thy shape
Of deities or mortals, or of both,
In Tempe or the dales of Arcady?
What men or gods are these? What maidens loath?
What mad pursuit? What struggle to escape?
What pipes and timbrels? What wild ecstasy?

Heard melodies are sweet, but those unheard
Are sweeter; therefore, ye soft pipes, play on;
Not to the sensual ear, but, more endeared,
Pipe to the spirit ditties of no tone:
Fair youth, beneath the trees, thou canst not leave
Thy song, nor ever can those trees be bare;

Bold Lover, never, never canst thou kiss,
Though winning near the goal—yet, do not grieve;
She cannot fade, though thou hast not thy bliss,
Forever wilt thou love, and she be fair!

Ah, happy, happy boughs! that cannot shed
Your leaves, nor ever bid the Spring adieu;
And, happy melodist, unwearièd,
Forever piping songs forever new;
More happy love! more happy, happy love!
Forever warm and still to be enjoyed,
Forever panting, and forever young;
All breathing human passion far above,
That leaves a heart high-sorrowful and cloyed,
A burning forehead, and a parching tongue.

Who are these coming to the sacrifice?
To what green altar, O mysterious priest,
Lead'st thou that heifer lowing at the skies,
And all her silken flanks with garlands dressed?
What little town by river or sea shore,
Or mountain-built with peaceful citadel,
Is emptied of its folk, this pious morn?
And, little town, thy streets forevermore
Will silent be; and not a soul, to tell
Why thou art desolate, can e'er return.

O Attic shape! Fair attitude! with brede
Of marble men and maidens overwrought,
With forest branches and the trodden weed;
Thou, silent form, dost tease us out of thought
As doth eternity: Cold Pastoral!

When old age shall this generation waste,
  Thou shalt remain, in midst of other woe
Than ours, a friend to man, to whom thou say'st,
"Beauty is truth, truth beauty,—that is all
  Ye know on earth, and all ye need to know."

I am ravished by that opening: "Thou still unravished bride of quietness." The urn is like a bride, married to quietness, forever a virgin, pure and untouched. "Still unravished" means "yet unravished," but also, of course, unmoving, "still." The first section describes the urn and claims that these silent images can express something better than words can. Keats addresses the urn, wondering if there is a story or legend behind the scene. Throughout the poem, asking questions of the urn, he thinks about how everything vanishes in life. Life, with its "breathing human passion far above, / That leaves a heart high-sorrowful and cloyed, / A burning forehead, and a parching tongue." Keats knew what he was talking about. He watched his mother, and later his brother Tom, die of tuberculosis—the disease that he would succumb to in a little house at the bottom of the Spanish Steps in Rome. One day, the poem says, everyone of this generation will be gone. Other people will replace them, but the urn will be the same. *Ars longa, vita brevis.*

Do you think that words can do more, or less, than a work of visual art? Are "more" and "less" the wrong terms? What about the idea that what we imagine—"unheard melodies"—is better than what actually exists? (Einstein said, "Imagination is better than reality.") Is it better that the Lover can't kiss his maiden, but she remains beautiful—or would you rather have him kiss her, and both of them grow old, as they might in life? (Or do you think they should live fast, die young, and leave beautiful corpses?) Near the end of his poem, Keats addresses the urn as a "Cold Pastoral." In the end he can't penetrate its mysteries; he can't know where the people leading that heifer in their ritual procession are coming from, and it seems that the poet, as much as the town he imagines, is "desolate." Always, when I read this poem, I feel taken into these paradoxes about art and life.

"Ode on a Grecian Urn" makes me think of a line by Sylvia Plath that makes a case for life: "Perfection is terrible, it cannot have children." Plath, though, committed suicide at thirty-two. Writing something isn't the same as living it.

Keats was powerfully affected by the questions his Grecian urn inspired. (Though he may have invented the urn as well, to illustrate his thinking.) No doubt you've encountered works of art that intrigue or compel you, that engage you at the level of your own questions about life. Try writing a poem in which you address or respond to such a painting, photograph, or sculpture.

First, here are a few more ekphrastic poems you can find online:

"Musée des Beaux Arts," W. H. Auden. After visiting the Museum of Fine Arts in Brussels, Auden wrote this poem, largely responding to *The Fall of Icarus* by the sixteenth-century Flemish painter Pieter Brueghel the Elder. The poem opens with the statement "About suffering they were never wrong, / The Old Masters." Brueghel's painting depicts people going about their daily activities onshore while the small figure of Icarus, the boy who flew too close to the sun, slips unnoticed beneath the waves. The ship in the painting, Auden says, "Had somewhere to get to and sailed calmly on." The poet finds in the painting a correspondence to his own vision of life.

"Landscape with the Fall of Icarus," William Carlos Williams. Williams, who wrote a series of poems based on Breughel's paintings, responded to *The Fall of Icarus* very differently; his spare poem is one of heartbreaking understatement, with no punctuation. One critic noted that the painting (which you're likely to encounter on the same web page as either Auden's or Williams's poem) portrays the view *from above*—it's what Icarus's father, Daedalus, would see, lagging behind his son who has flown exuberantly ahead of him, and higher, only to plummet into the sea. Williams captures this terrible perspective.

"Archaic Torso of Apollo," Rainer Maria Rilke. The last line of this poem is, "You must change your life." If you really let a work of art enter you, Rilke claims, it will change you. Though the head of the statue is missing, the poet says that "there is no place / that does not see you."

"The Tall Figures of Giacometti," May Swenson. Swenson has the sculptures speak to the viewer, describing themselves in a way that will remind you of Keats's paradoxes in "Ode on a Grecian Urn." These figures, though, are "ugly as truth is ugly." Write your own poem from the viewpoint of a sculpture, or the figure(s) in a drawing or painting.

For your own inspiration, besides reading the poems above, visit a museum. Look for a work of art that puts you under its spell. You could also choose a work of art that you respond to very negatively, and write about why you hate it. Bring your journal or laptop to the museum and sit where you can see the piece. Describe everything you see, as completely as possible. If a docent comes by with a group, listen in. Later, you might look up more information about the artwork or artist online. The image is your starting point, but let the poem travel from there.

10

read this

When I first read another Keats poem, "Ode to a Nightingale," I didn't understand it. I was blown away, and I didn't know why. "Was it a vision, or a waking dream? / Fled is that music:—Do I wake or sleep?"—those are the last lines of the poem. After reading them, I felt as though an electric current was running through me. I didn't know what certain words in the poem meant, like "Hippocrene." I didn't know exactly what Keats was saying about hearing this bird singing, or why, at one point, he wrote about wanting to die. Later, I memorized that poem because I loved it so much. As I memorized and reread it, more of its meanings unfolded. I understood the desire of the speaker to move out of himself and join the nightingale, to die into its seemingly timeless aria. Yet the poem still holds mystery for me—the mystery of what it was saying has become the mysterious nature of life itself, something I am brought back to each time I read the poem.

You don't have to understand something to be affected by it.

If you're new to reading poetry, don't worry if you don't get it. You'll get parts of a poem, and not others. Reading a poem several times helps. So does reading it aloud. Memorizing is even better. And once you know a few poems by heart, there will be occasions to say them. I have recited poems to bartenders and cabdrivers, to lovers and partygoers and bookstore audiences, to mourners at funerals. When I play tennis with a poet friend, we shout lines back and forth across the court. By taking poems into your body, you will get closer to them.

Books of poetry will teach you more than your mentor or professor or the well-known poet you have traveled to a conference to work with. Reading is like food to a writer; without it, the writer part of you will die—or become spindly and stunted. If you're afraid that reading will make you less original, don't be. Falling under the spell of—or reacting against—other writers is part of what will lead you to your own work. Reading in the long tradition of poetry shows you what has lasted, and those poems are there to learn from. Reading your contemporaries shows you what everyone else is up to in your own time, so you can map the different directions of the art. There's never one route to poetry, one style. Reading widely will help you see this.

Here is a sobering statistic: *Poetry*, which has been for many years one of the premier poetry journals in America, has about ten thousand subscribers. Every year, it receives ten times that many submissions from writers hoping to land a poem in its pages.

That's a hundred thousand people, writing.

Are they reading? Possibly. Maybe they're not subscribing to *Poetry* because they're spending their money on books by Neruda and Baudelaire and Muriel Rukeyser and Derek Walcott. But in fact, a large number of people who want to write poetry don't seem to like to read it. Many journals have a circulation of a few hundred copies, and poetry books sell dismally compared to fiction or memoir: the first print run is usually one or two thousand copies.

Maybe you're one of those people who writes poems, but rarely reads them. Let me put this as delicately as I can: If you don't read, your writing is going to suck.

Once, while visiting a university creative writing class, I was approached by a student who told me that he liked novels, but not poetry. "Interesting," I said. "How many poems have you read?" He said not many, but he'd been required to read a few for class and hadn't liked them. "Ever run into a novel you didn't like?" I asked him. "Well, yeah," he said.

It hadn't occurred to him that he could hate some poems or be indifferent to them, and still like poetry. He probably hadn't yet found poems that could matter to him. So he skipped poetry, and moved on.

If you want to write well, read. If you just want to be a poet the way some people want to be rock stars without actually learning the guitar, playing scales, and practicing—then you are free to fantasize.

When you read, read like a writer. For me this means that I am always paying attention, trying to solve a problem in my own work or pick up a new technique or move outward from what I already know. When I was trying to get a feel for long lines, I studied C. K. Williams. I took apart his sentences to understand their structure. I read and reread certain poems that spoke to me. I was like a medium, channeling a spirit. I had never met him, but he was one of my teachers. Every single writer I've read has taught me something. When people ask who my influences are, I can't answer. I'll mumble a name or two, and then a half dozen more, and stop. Otherwise I would go on forever.

Reading in this way doesn't dampen your enjoyment. When accomplished musicians listen to another player, they hear the notes differently than nonmusicians, with greater appreciation for the other player's skill. When you understand how sonnets work, you get more out of reading sonnets by Shakespeare or John Donne or Edna St. Vincent Millay or

Marilyn Nelson. You can see how they handled, beautifully, the challenges of the form.

I can't stress this point enough: You need to soak up as many books as you can. Even the ones you don't like can teach you something. If you were a painter, you'd spend time looking at works of art from every period in history. A chef I know, whenever he travels, eats enough for three people—he wants to sample all the dishes. Boxers study the great fights of the past, like the Ali-Forman "Thrilla in Manila." Marketers look at the successes of past products to try to duplicate those successes. Poetry isn't a product in that way, but you see what I mean. Read. Imitate shamelessly. Steal when you can get away with it. T. S. Eliot said, "Good poets imitate. Great poets steal."

So read. Let other writers teach and inspire you.

Unless you really want your writing to suck.

I got stoned in the kudzu
at William Faulkner's house
with my hosts from the university.

II.

inner and outer worlds

※ 11

identity 1: boys, girls & bodies

In the workshops I teach in my living room, there are almost always more women than men. I've often wondered why. Maybe men don't want to study with a woman. Maybe they'd rather learn alone than become part of a group. Once in fifteen years, there were more men than women, six to two, and the whole vibe of the workshop felt different. It's been shown in studies that in mixed-gender groups, women don't talk as much. We're trained to shut up. Men are trained to speak out.

I recently read a book on male depression that talked about how men tend to turn their depression outward, to damage others with anger and violence. Or else they cover it up. Women, on the other hand, damage themselves. Women are more likely to be cutters, to have eating disorders. So I'm thinking about how to explore gender in poems, and whether men and women really do write differently, as some theorists say. I'm not a theorist or a scholar. But it's logical that women and men would write differently, because writing is a function of who we are, and who we are partly has to do with being male or female. It has to do with how we were raised and the cultural messages we internalized before we even knew they were seeping in.

And then there is that part of us which is, in a larger sense, beyond gender. Call it soul, or spirit, or self: the *you* that happens to be residing in a body. If you believe there is nothing beyond the body, you probably still have a sense of what I'm talking about.

Poetry is not just about language, though language is its medium. Poetry's true subject is the spirit, the divine, the sacred, the ineffable. If you prefer God, use that word. It's just a word, though one that's loaded with baggage. And it makes poetry sound loftier than it is, since by God and the sacred I mean everything, the "what is" of life.

Art is about connecting to, and experiencing, the life of the spirit as it is lived in a physical body. This is what Whitman meant when he wrote in "Crossing Brooklyn Ferry," "I too had receiv'd identity by my body." Whitman was a great poet of both the physical self ("I am the poet of the woman the same as the man," he wrote) and the spirit. Here is the passage from which the line about identity comes:

5

What is it then between us?
What is the count of the scores or hundreds of years between us?

Whatever it is, it avails not—distance avails not, and place avails not,
I too lived, Brooklyn of ample hills was mine,
I too walk'd the streets of Manhattan island, and bathed in the waters
around it,
I too felt the curious abrupt questionings stir within me,
In the day among crowds of people sometimes they came upon me,

In my walks home late at night or as I lay in my bed they came upon
me,
I too had been struck from the float forever held in solution,
I too had receiv'd identity by my body,
That I was I knew was of my body, and what I should be I knew I
should be of my body.

In his time—the mid-nineteenth century—Whitman's poetry was considered shameful by many because of its frank depictions of the body. He didn't see the flesh as evil and the spirit as good; he saw the flesh *as* spirit. In his great work, *Leaves of Grass*, he creates a heroic self, "Walt Whitman, one of the roughs, a cosmos," connected to everyone and everything, passionately alive.

Here are lines taken from different sections of the opening to "Song of Myself" in *Leaves of Grass:*

The atmosphere is not a perfume, it has no taste of the distillation, it
is odorless,
It is for my mouth forever, I am in love with it,
I will go to the bank by the wood and become undisguised and naked,
I am mad for it to be in contact with me.

*

Urge and urge and urge,
Always the procreant urge of the world.

Out of the dimness opposite equals advance, always substance and
increase, always sex,
Always a knit of identity, always distinction, always a breed of life.

*

Welcome is every organ and attribute of me, and of any man hearty
and clean,
Not an inch nor a particle of an inch is vile, and none shall be less
familiar than the rest.

*

I believe in you my soul, the other I am must not abase itself to you,
And you must not be abased to the other.

So here you are, in a body, with a sexual identity—one that is part of your essential self, but also separate from it. You're a man or woman, or a person in between—gender, as it turns out, is a slippery slope. You think of yourself as gay or straight or bisexual, or you reject those words as labels. Use the following exercises to play with and explore what gender and gender roles mean to you.

indoctrinations

- When did you first realize what it meant to be a girl or boy? I remember the moment I was made to put on a T-shirt, after spending my early years as a happy shirtless savage running wild on the Florida beaches with my brothers. Maybe the realization arrived as you observed someone else—your mother dressing up to go out, a boy on the playground beaten up for acting "feminine." Write about that early experience.
- Write about a recent negative experience that seems related to your gender or to gender roles. Then write about a positive experience. This is tricky, because you can't always know the reasons behind how you are treated. But you can speculate. A woman friend of mine, a community college professor, was once physically intimidated by

some male students who wanted to be accepted into her overfull composition class. She doesn't think they would have acted that way toward a male professor; she thinks men receive more deference and are automatically granted authority.

- Make a list of activities you consider traditionally male or female. For example:

  fighting a war
  cleaning the toilet
  changing the baby's diapers
  washing the car

  If you are a woman, choose a "male" subject and describe yourself, or a woman, performing that action. If you are a man, do the reverse.
- For a group: Everyone bring in a passage of writing (prose is fine) that's unfamiliar; the aim is that no one know who the author is. Let everyone guess whether the writer is male or female and talk about why they came to that conclusion.
- When you were an adolescent, what did you think would "make you a man" or "make you a woman"? Write about your expectations of manhood/womanhood. What do you think now?
- An experience for men: Put on makeup, if you never have (or haven't since you were ten). Halloween doesn't count. Have your girlfriend or sister or another guy make you up. If you can, put on women's clothing. How does it feel? Write about it.
- An experience for women: Go out into the world looking your worst. Wear baggy pants, no makeup, don't brush your hair. Go into some place nice: a good restaurant, a high-end clothing store, a salon or spa. Write about it.
- Watch your favorite TV show or a movie and write down what you observe about the roles of men and women. Use the specifics of the characters and story.

- What did your father teach you about being a man? What did your mother teach you? How have you become a man like/unlike your father, a woman like/unlike your mother? You might want to make a list of things first, and then see if you can remember an event, or series of events, that really brought home to you some of these teachings.

"what do women want?"

This is the question Freud asked. I wrote a poem with that title (it's included in this book). It begins, "I want a red dress." A lot of people wrote to me about that poem. Women, especially, connected to the idea of claiming the power of their sexuality. Some saw the poem as being about freedom, and others felt it perpetuated the image of women as sex objects, and still others thought the mention of a burial at the end meant that women would always be imprisoned in certain roles. I think the poem can encompass all those ideas. It originated from a simple in-class exercise I gave my students at a community college: Begin with "I want," and see where the poem takes you.

For this exercise, focus on gender and desire. You might title your poem "What Women Want," or "What Men Want," and go from there. Or "What the [male or female body part here] Wants." Maybe you can spin it a bit differently: "I want a woman who . . ." "I want every man to . . ." "I wish I could . . ." "I love how you . . ." "What I really like . . ." Be playful, or serious, or ridiculous. Think about the ways we are taught to express, or suppress, our lust and desire. Here's a beautifully frank and unapologetic poem by Stephen Dobyns:

DESIRE

A woman in my class wrote that she is sick
of men wanting her body and when she reads

her poem out loud the other women all nod
and even some of the men lower their eyes

and look abashed as if ready to unscrew
their cocks and pound down their own dumb heads
with these innocent sausages of flesh, and none
would think of confessing his hunger

or admit how desire can ring like a constant
low note in the brain or grant how the sight
of a beautiful woman can make him groan
on those first days of spring when the parkas

have been packed away and the bodies are staring
at the bodies and the eyes stare at the ground;
and there was a man I knew who even at ninety
swore that his desire had never diminished.

Is this simply the wish to procreate, the world
telling the cock to eat faster, while the cock
yearns for that moment when it forgets its loneliness
and the world flares up in an explosion of light?

Why have men been taught to feel ashamed
of their desire, as if each were a criminal
out on parole, a desperado with a long record
of muggings, rapes, such conduct as excludes

each one from all but the worst company,
and never to be trusted, no never to be trusted?
Why must men pretend to be indifferent as if each
were a happy eunuch engaged in spiritual thoughts?

But it's the glances that I like, the quick ones,
the unguarded ones, like a hand snatching a pie
from a window ledge and the feet pounding away;
eyes fastening on a leg, a breast, the curve

of a buttock, as the pulse takes an extra thunk
and the cock, that toothless worm, stirs in its sleep,
and fat possibility swaggers into the world
like a big spender entering a bar. And sometimes

the woman glances back. Oh, to disappear
in a tangle of fabric and flesh as the cock
sniffs out its little cave, and the body hungers
for closure, for the completion of the circle,

as if each of us were born only half a body
and we spend our lives searching for the rest.
What good does it do to deny desire, to chain
the cock to the leg and scrawl a black X

across its bald head, to hold out a hand
for each passing woman to slap? Better
to be bad and unrepentant, better to celebrate
each difference, not to be cruel or gluttonous

or overbearing, but full of hope and self-forgiving.
The flesh yearns to converse with other flesh.
Each pore loves to linger over its particular story.
Let these seconds not be full of self-recrimination

and apology. What is desire but the wish for some
relief from the self, the prisoner let out

into a small square of sunlight with a single
red flower and a bird crossing the sky, to lean back

against the bricks with the legs outstretched,
to feel the sun warming the brow, before returning
to one's mortal cage, steel doors slamming
in the cell block, steel bolts sliding shut?

self-loathing, self-love

- Write a celebration of your sex: everything you love about men or women. Then write a celebration of the opposite sex.
- Write a condemnation of the opposite sex, then of your own. Let loose with everything that annoys you, bothers you, deeply disturbs you.
- Write a poem as a member of the opposite sex, praising your own; write a poem as a member of the opposite sex, condemning your own.
- Study yourself in a full-length mirror, naked. Write about what you love and what you hate about your body. Here's a poem of merciless and hilarious self-observation by Sharon Olds:

SELF PORTRAIT, REAR VIEW

At first, I do not believe it, in the hotel
triple mirror, that that is my body, in
back, below the waist, and above
the legs—the thing that doesn't stop moving
when I stop moving.
And it doesn't look like just one thing,
or even one big, double thing
—even the word saddlebags has a

smooth, calfskin feel to it,
compared to this compendium
of net string bags shaking their booty of
cellulite fruits and nuts. Some lumps
look like bonbons translated intact
from chocolate box to buttocks, the curl on top
showing, slightly, through my skin. Once I see what I can
do with this, I do it, high-stepping
to make the rapids of my bottom rush
in ripples like a world wonder. Slowly,
I believe what I am seeing, a 54-year-old
rear end, once a tight end,
high and mighty, almost a chicken butt, now
exhausted, as if tragic. But this is not
an invasion, my cul de sac is not being
used to hatch alien cells, ball peens,
gyroscopes, sacks of marbles. It's my hoard
of treasure, my good luck, not to be
dead, yet, though when I flutter
the wing of my ass again, and see,
in a clutch of eggs, each egg,
on its own, as if shelless, shudder, I wonder
if anyone has ever died,
looking in a mirror, of horror. I think I will
not even catch a cold from it,
I will go to school to it, to Butt
Boot Camp, to the video store, where I saw,
in the window, my hero, my workout jelly
role model, my apotheosis: Killer Buns.

⁂ 12

three meditations

Albert Camus once said that his writing was "a long journey to recover through the detours of art the two or three simple and great images that first gained access to my heart."

All of us have these images in our hearts. Our emotional lives are rich with the images of those we love. Our early experiences with love, and loss, are impressed on our imaginations. We go back over and over, in memory, to those experiences. They may be grand, life-changing events, or small moments filled with resonance. Philip Levine's "Starlight" describes a four-year-old boy standing with his father one evening, "on the porch of my first house." The father asks his son if he is happy, and the son, in that moment, understands something about his father's life. Years later, the adult narrator looks back on that quietly dramatic scene.

Looking back at our lives seems so much a part of our consciousness that we can rarely escape it. We obsess over the past, and spend so much time looking toward the future that we don't live our lives as they are, right now. As John Lennon said, "Life is what happens when you're making other plans." Living in the now is a worthy goal. But our memories, with all their attendant emotions, are an opportunity to take those "detours of art."

a place that used to be yours

Sit for a few minutes, eyes closed, and focus on a place where you once lived or spent a lot of time. Let your mind sort through a few possibilities until you settle on the one that feels most significant. That place might be a room, an apartment, an outdoor spot. It needs to be a place that once felt like yours, but that is now yours only in memory.

Revisit this place in your head. First, clearly visualize it. What do you see? Posters, furniture, a lake with a dock, a cornfield, pine trees and snow?

Listen to any sounds: birds, dishes clattering, TV, music.

Recall any tastes associated with that place: hot dogs at a ball game, candy at the movies, spinach, cough medicine, fruit punch.

Feel your surroundings: soft bed, stony ground, roof shingles.

What do you smell? Meat loaf, incense, pot smoke, perfume?

After you've virtually experienced your place, using all of your senses, open your eyes and write for ten minutes, describing the place in purely physical terms.

Now write about it emotionally for ten minutes. Were you happy, confused, miserable, all of those things at once?

Now write a third piece, without looking at the first two.

parent and child

Focus on an early memory that involves you and one or both of your parents: a day at the beach, riding in the back seat of the car on a trip, playing catch in the yard. The memory might be positive or negative, but it needs to be pivotal in some way. The memory should be one you associate with a lesson learned, a greater understanding of yourself or your parents or the world.

Again, close your eyes and visualize the scene. Imagine yourself into the physical location, through each of the five senses, so you are re-creating that place in vivid sensual detail.

Once you've done that, focus on your parent or parents in the scene. What did your mother or father sound like, smell like? Remember their clothing, gestures, words, in as much detail as possible.

Finally, focus on what happened between you and your parent(s). Let the memory enter you with all its particulars, all its emotional power.

Write for ten minutes, including not only what happened, but also the lesson you took from the experience.

lost & found love

Many couples tell stories about the moment when they first saw each other, or first fell in love. Meeting a love is a powerful moment. Parting from one is equally intense. Close your eyes and spend a few minutes remembering the highs and lows of those meetings and partings. Is there one experience, positive or negative, that you want to bring to the page? Spend a few more minutes focusing on that experience. The process, again, involves immersing yourself in the past and entering that prior experience before beginning to write.

When you write, be sure once again to include as much physical detail as possible.

You may want to do this exercise twice: once for a meeting or parting, and again for a meeting *and* parting. That is, take a relationship that didn't work out, and remember the beginning, and then the end, of that relationship.

A third possibility: Write about the ending of one relationship and the beginning of the next one.

⁜ 13

by heart: a love poem

The results of this exercise are meant for two people: you, and someone you love. Even if you're alone right now, learn a romantic poem for the day when you will have someone to say it to. Find a published poem that expresses your desires and feelings in a way that feels true and beautiful. Below are a few of my favorite love poems. Start with any of these, or find another that inspires you. If you are married or have a partner, surprise him or her with the poem on a special occasion. If one day you find yourself standing in front of friends and family vowing to love another person for life, for richer or poorer and all the rest, one of the following might come in handy.

Matthew Arnold, "Dover Beach"

Elizabeth Barrett Browning, Sonnet XIV from *Sonnets from the Portuguese*

E. E. Cummings, "somewhere I have never traveled, gladly beyond"

Robert Creeley, "For Love"

Emily Dickinson, "Wild Nights"

John Donne, "The Good-Morrow"

W. S. Merwin, "When You Go Away"

Edna St. Vincent Millay, Sonnet XXX from *Fatal Interview*

Pablo Neruda: Try poems from *Twenty Love Poems and a Song of Despair*, or the section "Love" from *The Captain's Verses*, or *100 Love Sonnets*

Kenneth Patchen, "As We Are So Wonderfully Done with Each Other"

Christina Rossetti, "Remember," "The First Day"

William Butler Yeats, "A Drinking Song," "The Ragged Wood," "When You Are Old"

14

love & sex poems

All poems are seductions. When you fall under the spell of a poem, it's an infatuation that can become a love affair. A poem wants you to feel like this; it doesn't feel complete unless it makes a personal connection. Some writers say they write only for themselves, but all writers want to reach readers. When you have a particular reader in mind, and he or she gives you arrhythmia, then you might want to write a love poem.

A boyfriend once left on my doorstep a rolled-up piece of drawing paper, tied with a ribbon, on which he'd copied excerpts from several poems, including this from Pablo Neruda: "I want to do with you what spring / does with the cherry trees." Needless to say, I called him right up.

I almost titled this chapter "Love Poems: How Not to Sound Like a Bad Hallmark Card." Full disclosure: I am a failed greeting-card writer.

When I was a twentysomething, broke, wannabe poet, I got this bright idea: I'd make money by selling clever lines to Hallmark. How hard could it be? I went to the library and found a book that instructed me to submit my work on 3-by-5-inch index cards. I went to Walgreens and lurked around the card aisle. Even then, I knew I had to read to be inspired. I bought the index cards, sent off what I thought were polished little gems, and waited for the money to roll in. I got a batch of form rejections, and my greeting-card dream died.

Especially in matters of the heart, the first language that comes to mind tends to be sappy, sentimental, and general. The language we reach for first is the language we know. It filters in from TV, movies, bad novels, greeting cards. This kind of language won't help you write a real poem (unless you make fun of it, which is called irony). For something better, you need some techniques. Reading will help you here.

The more you read, the more possibilities you will see.

For example, take Neruda's lines about the cherry trees. The cherry trees are a great metaphor. By imagining what happens to them in spring, we see and feel the poet's desire for his beloved. It would be bad, and corny, to say "I want to make you bloom like cherry blossoms in spring." Being that direct, in this case, wrecks the poetry. Neruda gives us the image to think about, and when we do, we get more from it than if he just tells us flat out. Sometimes being obvious is a real problem for writers. Sometimes the problem is the opposite, and no one can tell what the hell the writer is saying. You probably fall closer to one end of the continuum than the other. It's tricky to know when you should be more subtle, and when you need to be more direct. But you could take Neruda's lines as a point of departure, and fool with your own construction: *I want to do with you / what —— does to ——*. Or *I want to do with you / what a —— does to a ——*. I'll leave it to your imagination.

you

Write a detailed description of an object: a boat, a tree, a bottle, a shoe, etc. It doesn't matter what. The point is to make that object vivid and present for the reader.

After you've done this, begin a poem with "You are . . ." and imagine a loved one as that object. This is metaphor again—imagining one thing in terms of another. See if there are connections between your description of the object and your loved one. For example, you've written about a leaky rowboat. At first you might not see any connection. Maybe you see your lover more as a cruise ship. Use the first description anyway. Add the cruise ship for contrast, being as detailed as you were with the first description. Or imagine the lover might one day become a leaky rowboat. Or see how there is some part of your lover that is like a leaky rowboat, after all—everyone is wounded in some way. The point is to start from imagery and then see where the emotional intersections are.

Now try a different poem in which, rather than using one object as a metaphor, you list several. Here's my example:

You were a town with one pay phone and someone else was using it.
You were an ATM temporarily unable to dispense cash.
You were not responsible for any valuables left in my locked vehicle.
You were an outdated link and besides the server was down.
You were invisible to the naked eye.

From these lines, you can get a pretty good sense of the speaker's attitude toward this person. In your own poem, make the emotional meaning clear.

modern troubadour

The Troubadours were poet-musicians, who lived in the south of France between the eleventh and thirteenth centuries. They were especially known for their love poems, which were usually addressed to someone unattainable. In the tradition of courtly love, a nobleman would dedicate himself to loving a lady (or occasionally, vice versa)—often a married one.

You might want to update this convention by writing to someone who is unavailable. If he or she is married, proceed at your own risk. You could write to someone who seems unattainable for some other reason—a stranger, a celebrity. Courtly love was about an idealized version of intimacy.

Another kind of poem the troubadours wrote—though they didn't invent it—was the *aubade*, or dawn song. The convention of the aubade is this: Dawn is coming. The lovers have to part. (Maybe, in the case of some of the troubadors, because the husband was arriving soon?) The aubade often took the form of a dialogue between the lovers. *Romeo and Juliet* contains a well-known passage in which, after spending the night together in Juliet's bed, the lovers hear a bird outside. Juliet insists that it's a nightingale—so they still have time to stay together—while Romeo claims he hears a lark, announcing the break of day.

Two post-troubadour aubades are John Donne's "The Sun Rising," which opens:

> Busy old fool, unruly Sun,
> Why dost thou thus,
> Through windows, and through curtains, call on us?
> Must to thy motions lovers' seasons run?
> Saucy pedantic wretch, go chide
> Late school-boys and sour prentices,
> Go tell court-huntsmen that the king will ride,
> Call country ants to harvest offices;

Love, all alike, no season knows nor clime,
Nor hours, days, months, which are the rags of time.

—and Philip Larkin's "Aubade," which begins, "I work all day and get half-drunk at night." There is no lover in Larkin's poem; the speaker is alone, awake and alone at 4 A.M., feeling a deep sense of dread about the chilling fact of death. Eventually the morning comes, but the day brings only the clarity of knowing "that we can't escape, / Yet can't accept." His is an anti-aubade. Write your own aubade, one that either follows the conventions or resists them.

love rules

Here are some poets' words on romantic love:

Love is not love / Which alters when it alteration finds.

—William Shakespeare, Sonnet 116

Lovers don't finally meet each other along the road. They're in each other all along.

—Rumi, "My First Love Story"

Love bears all things, believes all things, hopes all things, endures all things.

—1 Corinthians 13:7

Till I loved / I never lived—Enough.

—Emily Dickinson, 549

Love consists in this, that two solitudes protect and touch and greet each other."

—Rainer Maria Rilke, Letters to a Young Poet

> Being deeply loved by someone gives you strength, while loving someone deeply gives you courage.
>
> —*Lao Tzu*

Using one of these as a starting point, explore your own ideas about love. Agree, argue, or take any of the excerpts above further. What in your experience or observation has led to your conclusions about love? Include the evidence that backs up your ideas.

love stinks

Love gone bad: What does that look like? Sour milk, a dead or dying animal, rotting plums, a casino under the wrecking ball? Charles Bukowski wrote, "Love is a dog from hell." Write about a relationship that didn't work out, developing one or several images. You might formulate your own "Love is . . ." as a way to begin.

i love you—not

Write an ironic "I love you" poem: I love the way you never return my phone calls, I love you when you invite me to a party and ignore me all evening, I love the HPV you gave me. When your ex calls in the middle of the night about nothing—a spider in the bathroom—and you jump out of our bed and run right over, wow, then I really love you.

i hate & love

The Roman poet Catullus, born around 84 B.C., died when he was about thirty. To read Catullus is to go back to the source of a lot of love poetry.

Catullus could write lovely lines and extremely graphic ones as well. When you read his work, you feel you are hearing a living person speaking from the page. Though Catullus lived so long ago, his poems express emotions that are familiar to us. The human body today is the same as it was two thousand years ago—and so, apparently, is the human heart. Here's a brief Catullus poem:

POEM 85

I hate & love. And if you should ask how I can do both,
I couldn't say; but I feel it, and it shivers me.
(translated by Charles Martin)

Catullus wrote many poems to a woman he called Lesbia, who was probably a married woman named Claudia. Here's another:

POEM 72

You used to say that you wished to know only Catullus,
  Lesbia, and wouldn't take even Jove before me!
I didn't regard you just as my mistress then: I cherished you
  as a father does his sons or his daughters' husbands.
Now that I know you, I burn for you even more fiercely,
  though I regard you as almost utterly worthless.
How can that be, you ask? It's because such cruelty forces
  lust to assume the shrunken place of affection.
(translated by Charles Martin)

If someone you loved ever said to you, "You're great, I really like you, but I just want to be friends now," you can probably relate to this poem. Write about your ambivalent feelings about someone. But first, go online and read "Hate Poem" by Julie Sheehan, which wittily captures that love-hate dynamic.

the joy of sex

The sex manual *The Joy of Sex* was published in 1972 and was a huge best-seller. In 2002, Elizabeth Benedict wrote *The Joy of Writing Sex.* It's directed to fiction writers, but is useful for poets as well. Benedict talks about "hiring a decorator"—creating a vivid setting for your characters to connect (or not—another thing she reminds us is that not all sex is good sex). I've read hundreds of poems about sex in which the bodies seem to float in space, with no context. No black satin or stained sheets, no incense or candles or neon sign flickering through the window, no Coltrane or Dresden Dolls from the next room, no pillows pushed to the floor, no floor.

Context helps you to be more specific; it can also reinforce mood, like the lighting of candles. Say, fifty tea lights set around the room. Read Galway Kinnell's "Last Gods," which places us beside a lake with two naked lovers. Paul Blackburn's "The Once-Over" is about imagined sex—the lustful glances a blond woman receives—and puts us "in the center of the subway car," detailing the inhabitants and train route in New York City. In that case, setting is used for contrast—the sexual breaking through the mundane. Sharon Olds's sex poems are rich in setting: a hot tub, a bathroom, a floor with a braided rug.

Try both kinds of poem—one in which you create a context that mirrors the mood, and one in which you have, say, a cheap motel setting but transcendent sex.

what to call it

It's helpful to think of the people in your poems as characters. That gives you some distance, which is a good thing. Sometimes, distance can free you to write what you might not otherwise say. Putting a sex poem in the third person can also be liberating: "he" or "she" might do things that "I" would be uncomfortable with. Benedict has some useful advice on this, too: Call something what your characters would call it.

The identification of body parts is fascinating. Certain words can trigger strong feelings. The word "cunt," for example, from the Middle English *cunte.* It's going to summon up something different from "vagina," or "her sex," or—here's a hilarious one—"her fuzzy coin purse."

For some people, "cunt" is sexy; for many it's demeaning. "Vagina" sounds clinical, but you may feel differently if you've seen Eve Ensler's theater piece, *The Vagina Monologues.* In Florida, some citizens complained about the V-word displayed on a theater marquee. (It was changed briefly to *The Hoo-Hah Monologues.* Eventually the theater was allowed to reinstate the original title.) "Her sex" is a phrase Sharon Olds has used, which strikes me as fairly neutral. Depending on your poem, it might be too neutral.

The words you use to describe sex can affect the entire tone of your poem. Go carefully into the territory of the explicit. If you use a word like "fuck," make sure it's the best, most accurate word. If you use a Latinate word, recognize that it may be distancing. If you choose Victorian euphemisms like "his helmet of steel," I hope you're trying to crack up your reader.

We could use a few more humorous sex poems, so try some outrageous euphemisms of your own.

celebrating eros

Eros, the Greek god of love, is associated not only with sex but with creativity, with fertility and the life force. This poem by Charles Harper Webb begins with sex (and death), entertains some clever metaphors (the penis "nude, without a raincoat," the womb "full as a World Cup stadium"), and careens giddily through the world as the speaker's son is being born:

PRAYER TO TEAR THE SPERM-DAM DOWN

Because we need to remember / that memory will end, let the womb remain / untouched.

—FROM "PRAYER TO SEAL UP THE WOMBDOOR" BY SUZANNE PAOLA

Because we know our lives will end,
Let the vagina host a huge party, and let the penis come.

Let it come nude, without a raincoat.
Let it come rich, and leave with coffers drained.

Throw the prostate's floodgates open.
Let sperm crowd the womb full as a World Cup stadium.

Let them flip and wriggle like a mackerel shoal.
Let babies leap into being like atoms after the Big Bang.

Let's celebrate fullness, roundness, gravidity.
Let's worship generation—this one,

And the next, and next, forever.
Let's adore the progression: protozoan to guppy

To salamander to slow loris to Shakespeare.
Forget Caligula. Forget Hitler. Mistakes

Were made. Let's celebrate our own faces
Grinning back at us across ten thousand years.

Let's get this straight: Earth doesn't care if it's overrun—
If it's green or brown or black, rain forest, desert, or ice pack.

A paper mill is sweet as lavender to Earth,
Which has no sense of smell, and doesn't care

If roads gouge it, or industries fume into its air.
Beetles don't care. Or crows,

Or whales, despite their singing and big brains.
Sure, rabbits feel. Spicebush swallowtails

Feel their proboscides slide into flowers'
Honeypots, which may feel too,

But lack the brains to care. Even if beagles
Are as mournful as they look—

Even if great apes grieve, wage war, catch termites
With twigs, and say in sign language,

"Ca-ca on your head," they still don't care.
Or if they do—well, join the club.

We humans care so much, some of us dub life
A *vale of tears*, and see heaven as oblivion.

Some pray, for Earth's sake, not to be reborn.
Wake up! Earth will be charred by the exploding sun,

Blasted to dust, reduced to quarks, and still not care.
If some people enjoy their lives too much

To share, let them not share. If some despise themselves
Too much to reproduce, let them disappear.

If some perceive themselves as a disease, let them
Take the cure, and go extinct. It's immaterial to Earth.

Let people realize this, or not. Earth doesn't care.
I do, and celebrate my own fecundity.

I celebrate my wife's ovaries, her fallopian tubes
Down which, like monthly paychecks,

Gold eggs roll. I celebrate the body's changing.
(Might as well; it changes anyway.)

I celebrate gestation, water breaking,
The dash to the hospital, the staff descending,

Malpractice policies in hand. I celebrate
Dilation of the cervix, doctors in green scrubs,

And even (since I won't get one) the episiotomy.
I'll celebrate my bloody, dripping son, head deformed

By thrusting against the world's door.
Let it open wide for him. Let others make room for him.

Let his imagination shine like God's.
Let his caring change the face of everything.

Where do you find the evidence of the world's persistent creativity, and the desire of things in the world to join and merge? Praise it, pray. Write a poem in celebration of Eros.

⁂ 15

me, myself & i

When you explore your own life in poetry, it's useful to remember that nobody really cares. Nobody, that is, but your parents, your pals on Facebook, and your best friend. Your life is fascinating to you and—possibly—a handful of other people. You are the hero of your drama, the center of your own universe. But so is everyone else. If you want a reader's attention, you've got to be interesting.

Gertrude Stein said that she wrote "for myself and strangers." Remember that strangers have their own lives and loves and failures to care about. Like other kinds of poems, the poem of personal experience can be done very well, but is often done badly. Usually this is because the writer is more focused on his or her own personal experience than on the making of a poem.

The bottom line here is that you aren't the only one who has lost someone, or been hurt, or been so in love you felt like your body was pulsing with light. Even if you are very talented, or very beautiful, blessed or cursed in ways most of us aren't—you're just one among the many. This has an upside: you aren't special, but you are unique. No one but you can express what you have to express. Dancer and choreographer Martha Graham put it this way:

> There is a vitality, a life force, an energy, a quickening, that is translated through you into action, and because there is only one of you in all time, this expression is unique.

the "apparently personal"

Many poems written in the first person seem to describe the actual experiences of the poets themselves. A poet writes of an abortion or love affair, or describes spending a night in jail, or standing by the bedside of an ailing parent; we can identify and sympathize, or learn something about an experience we might not have had. Yet poets, while seeking to reveal truths, are not always faithful to the facts. Picasso said, "Art is a lie that makes us realize the truth." I like to think of it this way: The page is a kind of stage. When you step onstage, you become a character. When you write a first-person poem, you also become a character, even if you are describing actual events from your life.

The "I" on the page might be analytical in one poem and over-the-top emotional in another. The writer might be a slightly better—or worse—person in daily life. And he or she might be inventing everything, pretending sincerity. Does this mean that poets can't be trusted? In a sense, yes, if you read poems for facts. But poets do try to be true to life's mystery and complexity, and in order to do that, they—and you, if you want to be truthful—need to invent.

Sharon Olds speaks of first-person poems about intimate events as the "apparently personal." Asked about a poem in which the speaker forgave her father, a difficult, abusive man who appears in much of her work, she responded, "Oh, I didn't forgive him. I only wrote that I did." And of course the "I" of the poem, assumed to be Olds, may not have been.

Let me give you an example from my own work. This is from my fourth book of poems, *What Is This Thing Called Love.* It's loosely in the form of a blues poem—two repeating lines, with a third line that rhymes. The couple in the poem is on a trip to Italy that is anything but romantic:

BLUES FOR DANTE ALIGHIERI

. . . without hope we live on in desire . . .
—INFERNO, IV

Our room was too small, the sheets scratchy and hot—
Our room was a kind of hell, we thought,
and killed a half-liter of Drambuie we'd bought.

We walked over the Arno and back across.
We walked all day, and in the evening, lost,
argued and wandered in circles. At last

we found our hotel. The next day we left for Rome.
We found the Intercontinental, and a church full of bones,
and ate takeout Chinese in our suite, alone.

It wasn't a great journey, only a side trip.
It wasn't love for eternity, or any such crap;
it was just something that happened . . .

We packed suitcases, returned the rental car.
We packed souvenirs, and repaired to the airport bar
and talked about pornography, and movie stars.

If you take this poem at face value and consider the person telling this story—me, supposedly—you'd think I had a terrible time on this trip. You'd probably say I'm bitter about this guy, and wrote this poem to express that bitterness.

You'd be wrong.

In fact, it was a great trip. Many of the details in the poem are accurate—we did stay in a tiny hotel room in Florence, and got lost in that city. In Rome, we visited "a church full of bones"—the Capuchin Cemetery, where the monks had sorted the bones of their departed brethren and used them to create chandeliers and other unnerving but compelling sculptures. We ate takeout Chinese—twice—because we had been gorging on Italian food and needed a break. We had a fabulous time. I made up the parts about drinking Drambuie in our hotel room, and arguing when we were lost. Our love was a very good one; we were living together at the time. There was no rental car. And I haven't a clue what we talked about at the airport.

What interested me, while writing the poem, was an idea sparked by the quote from Dante. The *Inferno* is a brilliant work and a fascinating read. Politics, religion, torture—just like modern times. My idea was this: So what about love? What if lasting love really is impossible, but we keep wanting and needing it anyway? That's a kind of hell. So I used this lovely trip I had taken with this great guy, and I made it sound much worse than it was. I wanted the truth of the idea, and so I created this other person, this "I" and not-I. I wanted a sense of doomed hope—not the fun of hanging out in a classy hotel in Rome, drinking delicious wine with our cartons of Chinese food. And I wanted to end with the word "stars," because that's what Dante did, in all three books of the *Divine Comedy*. But I wanted my stars not to be beacons of transcendence; I wanted them profane. So I came up with pornography and movie stars.

This may give you some insight into how and why poets invent in their work, and how you can do the same. By the way, if you are interested in writing blues poems, an excellent source of inspiration is the recent anthology *Blues Poems*, compiled by Kevin Young. You can also find a discussion of blues poems in *The Poet's Companion*, and in Muriel Rukeyser's generous, wide-ranging book of essays, *The Life of Poetry*.

my selves

We all play multiple roles in daily life. You may talk baby talk to your cat and be officious on the phone at work. In one day you may be a student, a mother or father, a lover, a best friend, a customer, a member of a club, a stranger on the street. Exploring these selves—present, past, and those you may become—can help you move away from thinking of the "I" in your poem as *you yourself*, and toward "I" as a character or a version of you.

Try this exercise: List your various selves, including your (their) hopes and fears. Here is my list. It includes not only selves, but some sort of action or situation:

PAST
The Catholic girl takes her first Communion
The teenager fights with her father over doing the dishes
The college dropout moves to California
The secretary lies to her boss
PRESENT
The writer stares out the window, admiring her red curtains
The trapeze student climbs the ladder
The harmonica player at the open mike
The tenant complains to her landlord
FUTURE (hopes)
The National Book Award winner thanks her mother
The poet becomes a grandmother
FUTURE (fears)

The burn victim at the morgue
The old woman breaks her hip
The blind woman addresses her cane

Make your own list. When you're finished, you're likely to have titles and subjects for several poems. Then go ahead and speak in the first person, as one of your selves. Use your life as material, to tell some truth. But don't let your poem be confined by facts.

i feel . . .

In 1997, Hervé Le Tellier wrote *Mille pensées*, "one thousand thoughts," with each line beginning, "I think . . ." In 2005, Denise Duhamel wrote a book of a thousand and one lines, each beginning, "I feel . . ." Some of the "I feel"s seem to be true of Denise Duhamel, the writer, but others clearly aren't. Still others are based on wordplay, like a series of alphabetical "I feel . . ." statements beginning with "I feel amorous around angels." Here's an excerpt from her book *Mille et un sentiments*:

71. I feel like shoplifting small things sometimes.
72. I feel angry at myself when I don't meet my goals.
73. I feel like no one even cares what my goals are but me.
74. I feel self-centered—I feel like putting on my favorite hat, the one that I designed myself, the one with the mirror hanging from its brim so I can constantly look into my own eyes.
75. I feel bad when he tells me I'm too self-centered.
76. I feel as though I should work more on being less self-centered.
77. I feel no more than 77 percent of any list poem should be autobiographical.
78. I feel as though no one respects me because I'm a go-go dancer.
79. I feel like being pushed against the wall, then spanked.

80. I feel like going topless everywhere—that's how much I like myself.
81. I feel as though if you knew I had both a penis and a vagina, you might not want to date me. Is this true?
82. I feel as though everyone should admire my Rolex.
83. I feel as though the Porsche we just bought might be a little too flashy.

Write an "I feel . . ." or an "I think . . ." or an "I believe . . ." or an "I remember . . ." poem. Play with the "I" that is you, and the "I" that is not you.

the person in *persona*

Persona is Latin for "mask." In a *persona* poem, the "I" is more obviously a character. T. S. Eliot's "The Love Song of J. Alfred Prufrock" is spoken by a fearful, aging man who says, "I grow old . . . I grow old . . . / I shall wear the bottoms of my trousers rolled." William Carlos Williams's "The Widow in Springtime" is a heartbreaking portrayal of a woman who tells us, "Sorrow is my own yard," and who wishes to die, herself, after losing her husband of thirty-five years. "The Good Shepherd," by Ai, is a chilling poem that doesn't flinch from inhabiting the mind of a serial killer. Read these poems, and you'll see, even from this small sampling, how poets create memorable characters whose circumstances are far from their own lives.

Using a *persona* is a way to explore the world through a different lens. It's a great tool when you want distance from your life story. New poets tend to start with their own stories; many never move away from them. Your own life story *may* be all the territory you need to cover. But the strategy of creating a *persona* is worth looking at—not only as a way to enter other lives, but also as a way to map your *inner* territory.

The truth is, you will be in your work with or without an obvious *persona*. William Carlos Williams was not a woman and had not lost his spouse, but we know from "The Widow in Springtime" that he was sensitive to grief, that he thought deeply about its effects. As a physician, he was familiar with death and loss. Adopting a *persona* is a way into your own profound questions and concerns. In a *persona* poem, you can become an actor and enter the page as anyone—rock star, grandparent, space alien—and investigate the things that matter most to you.

Jot down your ideas for creating a *persona*. You might speak as a comic book hero, a mythological or historical figure. Philip Levine's amazing poem "Animals Are Passing from Our Lives" is in the voice of a pig. It may help to place your character in a situation or setting right away. Ai's poem begins, "I lift the boy's body / from the trunk," a horrific and powerful opening that takes us immediately into the reality of the killer. Whatever *persona* you choose, infuse it with your own sensibilities, your own urgencies.

16

what you don't know

One doesn't discover new lands without consenting to lose sight of the shore for a very long time.

—*André Gide*

The ability to begin, and then sustain, any kind of creative work means being able to tolerate ambiguity and uncertainty. Confusion and questioning are part of the creative process for all writers, at all levels. And, of course, they are an integral part of life. We don't know where our lives are going, or who we are becoming. We may remember the person we once were, and the things that person did, with a sense of disbelief.

Li-Young Lee captures the mystery of the self in this quietly precise lyric. The speaker doesn't have any answers to the mystery; he simply renders the truth of that awareness, his "unknowing":

EVENING HIEROGLYPH

Birds keep changing places in the empty tree
like decimals or numerals reconfiguring

some word which, spoken, might sound the key
that rights the tumblers in the iron lock
that keeps the gate dividing me from me.

Late January. The birds face all
one direction and flit
from branch to branch.

They raise no voice
against or for oncoming dark, no answer
to questions asked by one
whose entire being seems a question

posed to himself, one no longer new
on earth, unknowing, and yet,
still not the next thing.

When my daughter moved to New York after college, she faced the uncertainty of finding a job, a place to live, negotiating the city. She had moved there to become an actor (which often means actor/waitperson), and wondered if she had made the right decision. I sent her this passage from Rainer Maria Rilke's *Letters to a Young Poet:*

> Have patience with everything that remains unsolved in your heart. Try to love the questions themselves, like locked rooms and like books written in a foreign language. Do not now look for the

> answers. They cannot now be given to you because you could not live them. It is a question of experiencing everything. At present you need to live the question. Perhaps you will gradually, without even noticing it, find yourself experiencing the answer, some distant day.

"To live the question" is great—and difficult—advice.

Keats called the ability to do this "Negative Capability": "that is when a man is capable of being in uncertainties, Mysteries, doubts, without any irritable reaching after fact & reason." The poetic state of mind isn't grasping. It isn't passive, either. Receptive may be a better word.

Often, poems are not about what their writers know, but what they don't know. A poem can open a field of inquiry. If you know too much when you start out, your poem may fail because there is nothing to discover. You've closed all the doors, in advance, for yourself and your reader.

One way to make discoveries is to ask questions. Elizabeth Bishop's "In the Waiting Room" shows us a young girl studying the photos in a *National Geographic* magazine, who finds herself taken into a whirlpool of questions about her own identity. In another of Bishop's poems, "Filling Station," the questions are more practical than existential, but the speaker's curiosity enables us to discover, with her, the nature of the family that runs the "dirty," "oil-permeated" filling station, and beautifies it.

Consider, too, this poem by William Wordsworth:

SURPRISED BY JOY

Surprised by joy—impatient as the Wind
I turned to share the transport—Oh! with whom
But Thee, deep buried in the silent tomb,
That spot which no vicissitude can find?
Love, faithful love, recalled thee to my mind—
But how could I forget thee? Through what power,

Even for the least division of an hour,
Have I been so beguiled as to be blind
To my most grievous loss!—That thought's return
Was the worst pang that sorrow ever bore,
Save one, one only, when I stood forlorn,
Knowing my heart's best treasure was no more;
That neither present time, nor years unborn
Could to my sight that heavenly face restore.

The speaker has a moment of happiness, turns to share it with someone who has died, and realizes that for that moment of happiness, he had forgotten his grief. How could he have forgotten the person "deep buried in the silent tomb," even for a minute? This passionate, agonized question drives the speaker to grieve all over again.

Once you're tuned in to questions in poetry, they seem to be everywhere. *Shall I compare thee to a summer's day? And how shall I presume? How do they do it, the ones who make love without love? Of those so close beside me, which are you? What happens to a dream deferred? Why is it no one ever sent me yet / one perfect limousine, do you suppose? America when will we end the human war? Is there—is there balm in Gilead? / —tell me—tell me, I implore! Who would be a turtle who could help it? And hast thou slain the Jabberwock?*

William Blake's "The Tyger" makes its way entirely through questioning:

Tyger! Tyger! burning bright
In the forests of the night,
What immortal hand or eye
Could frame thy fearful symmetry?

In what distant deeps or skies
Burnt the fire of thine eyes?

On what wings dare he aspire?
What the hand dare seize the fire?

And what shoulder, & what art
Could twist the sinews of thy heart?
And when thy heart began to beat,
What dread hand? & what dread feet?

What the hammer? what the chain?
In what furnace was thy brain?
What the anvil? what dread grasp
Dare its deadly terrors clasp?

When the stars threw down their spears,
And water'd heaven with their tears,
Did he smile his work to see?
Did he who made the Lamb make thee?

Tyger! Tyger! burning bright
In the forests of the night,
What immortal hand or eye
Dare frame thy fearful symmetry?

Blake's tyger, or tiger, is an awesome creature, and the first question Blake asks is, What God could "frame," or create, this terrifying animal? Though the question is addressed to the tiger, it's a question about God. And about what one might called the "experience" side of life instead of the "innocence" side. ("The Tyger" can be found in Blake's *Songs of Experience.* Its companion poem, "The Lamb," appears in his *Songs of Innocence.*) The tiger seems always to have been there, flaming, burning, its energy wrenched into form with hammer and anvil. And then the question, *Did he smile his work to see?* Was God pleased, and could the same

God that created this animal have also made the lamb—the animal that represents meekness? *Lamb* is also Jesus, "the Lamb of God": the sacrifice. Or the one eaten by the tiger. Innocence and experience, prey and predator, good and evil, the nature of a world that contains both—all of these are encompassed by the series of questions that circle back and never truly offer answers. The most we could say is that they are answered in a limited sense—yes, the tiger and the lamb were both made by the same "immortal hand." But the deeper question, the paradox of both things existing, remains. How can the world be so terrible and beautiful at once? Why is it all creation and destruction at the same time? Those are some of my own questions that return whenever I read this poem.

a burning question

In "The Tyger," Blake asks a question he can't really answer. Begin a poem with an important question of your own that you can't answer. Then, keep asking questions as a way to explore the topic and move the poem forward.

a rhetorical question

Want to know one of my favorite rhetorical questions in poetry? It's from Whitman's *Song of Myself*:

> Do I contradict myself?
> Very well then I contradict myself;
> (I am large, I contain multitudes.)

In a poem about the death of her friend the poet Anne Sexton, Maxine Kumin begins by addressing her, "Shall I say how it is in your clothes?"

Rhetorical questions like these give you a way to introduce your subject; you can ask the question and then answer it. The uncertainties here won't be in the questions themselves. You'll have to let them give way to other surprises and mysteries. In Kumin's poem "How It Is," the speaker is stunned by the ordinary, mundane objects that survive—the friend's jacket, a parking ticket in the pocket—in the face of overwhelming loss. The larger question here is how the poet can possibly come to terms with the loss, how she can "put on the dumb blue blazer of your death."

i am clueless

Consider something you *really* don't know about: You have no idea how you could join the conversation if this came up. Type your topic—string theory, whale migration, Norse mythology—into a search engine, find some interesting or surprising facts, and make a poem out of your new knowledge.

i want to know

When my brother had to undergo a liver transplant, I watched a slide show online during his operation in order to understand what was happening. Later I used some of what I learned in a poem.

Think of what is happening in the life of a friend or family member or neighbor right now. The idea is to re-create what someone close to you is experiencing. You might research someone's illness, or learn more about a city a friend is visiting. Maybe your sister is pregnant and you want to know exactly what happens during childbirth. Focus on another person's experience, and after answering some of your own questions, try to enter that experience.

now I know

We know that tragic events are happening in other places, but in a sense we don't know. Because we (most of us, at least) aren't physically there, it's easier to keep these events at the edges of our consciousness. A certain amount of denial is necessary; if you went around 24/7 aware of all the suffering in the world, you'd lose your sanity. We need filters. But it can become tempting to filter too much, to ignore difficulty and avoid intensity.

The truth is, life is difficult and intense.

The beauty is that we have art and love to give us solace, and joy, a reason to live and a reason to care about what happens in, and to, the world.

So these two exercises are about looking at something you haven't been aware of, or have kept at the edges of your awareness. It's challenging to write about distant events, so the point of doing these exercises is to bring them closer.

1. Read today's *New York Times*, in print or online. Also visit these news sites, and any others you know of:

    http://www.commondreams.org
    http://www.counterpunch.org
    http://www.thenation.com
    http://www.crooksandliars.com

    As you read, jot down the words and phrases that make you feel emotion—sadness, anger, outrage, pity, relief, fear. Imagine the people who are affected by these events. Forget the corporations or the bills being passed through the legislature. Focus on the human story.

    This poem by Susan Browne takes off from a headline, and uses a heavy dose of irony as a strategy for dealing with the horrific. The distance between the speaker's upbeat, cheerful response and the reality of the news creates a powerful dissonance:

TWO CLERICS HACKED TO DEATH IN HOLY CITY

I just love that, so let me say it again.
The alliteration alone is admirable, and the cadence—
nothing better than iambic pentameter:
Two Clerics Hacked to Death in Holy City.

Man, that's got swing, ring-a-ding, and an action
verb. I can really feel it, *hack*, I can almost see it,
hack, hack, hack. Talk about a wake-up call.
This morning, I'm reading the news, checking in
with the war when like music to my ears:

Two Clerics Hacked to Death in Holy City.
It should win the Pulitzer, or maybe
the Nobel. But then I turn the page,
and listen to this:

A Five-Year-Old Aims His Kalashnikov.
Such lovely triple rhythms! A natural progression,
and I can't wait to hear tomorrow's song:
the harmonics of humanity, the croon
of carnage in every holy city.

2. I've listed some online sites that show graphic photographic evidence of tragic events and circumstances. One of your challenges here—beyond the real challenge of looking at these images—is to move beyond what I call "button-pushing" in your writing. To say

"dead child" or "concentration camp" is to push a button. We can't help but respond emotionally to certain words or phrases, but the poem can't rely on those to make us feel. It has to do the work of finding a shape.

The pitfalls here are many. The tendency of most writers is to be too earnest or melodramatic. Aiming for intensity, they end up producing what someone called "poetic necrophilia," exploiting other people's misery. Generally, it's best to work against the power of disturbing images as a way, paradoxically, to examine them. Susan Browne's poem demonstrates that tone is an effective strategy; where we expect outrage, we get mock aesthetic appreciation. Elsewhere in this book, you'll find more ways to tackle such subject matter: metaphor, understatement, the use of other narratives such as myths and fairy tales. For now, it may be enough to "check in" with the grimmer facts of the world. But don't do this until and unless you are prepared to be unsettled.

- http://www.terra.com.br/sebastiaosalgado
  (Sebastião Salgado, 1980s famine in Africa)
- http://www.exploratorium.edu/nagasaki/journey/journey1.html
  (Yosuke Yamahata, photographs and text about the bombing of Nagasaki, 1945)
- http://www.dahrjamailiraq.com/gallery/albums.php
  (photographs from Iraq, Syria, Lebanon, and the Middle East)
- http://www.shamash.org/holocaust/photos
  (photographs of the Holocaust)
- http://www.armeniapedia.org/index.php?title=Armenian_Genocide_Photos
  (photographs of the Armenian genocide)
- http://www.ushmm.org/conscience/alert/darfur/steidle
  (photographs and text about Darfur)

17

three observations

Training our awareness is important, not only for writing, but for experiencing life moment to moment. Here is an observation exercise I do daily—not as discipline, but to alleviate boredom. I do this exercise when I am standing in line at the DMV or grocery store, or walking to get somewhere, or otherwise experiencing what used to be dead time. Before, my thoughts would turn on themselves, like a cat licking and licking its fur, obsessively grooming. Now I simply say to myself: Three things. Look around, observe three things that are striking or unusual, and note them. (I write them down, though I can't always do it at the time.)

Doing this makes the environment immediately more interesting. On long car trips with our parents, my brothers and I used to play the game that went, "I spy, with my little eye . . . something blue." Or green. Or beginning with *c*. One of my brothers would try to find that object, and then we'd switch roles. It was a way to kill time, a distraction from the fact that we weren't there yet. But it was also a way to tune in to what was around us, to take in the world.

Odd signs, bumper stickers, strange behavior—note anything unusual or just plain vivid. A man walking backwards through a door. A tree filled with pairs of shoes. The pizzeria in the Mission (a largely Hispanic and Latino district in San Francisco) where the Chinese man is cooking Italian food while mariachis play. Translation of world to word.

My three items this morning, while I was walking to the train, were these: a smashed yellow Caspar's Hot Dogs cup; a sign on a run-down building, optimistically titled SPA, with the words *Hair Models Wanted*; a sanitation worker who jumped from an enormous, noisy truck and ran to pick up a pair of dirty work gloves from a doorway. These things may not sound promising as material for poetry, but any of them might mysteriously become the right detail to enter a poem—or start it—in the future. They are three details of the material world that I would otherwise not have noticed. I could have told you that I passed storefronts, that there was litter on the sidewalk, that there was a truck, but I would not have really *seen* them.

The point of this exercise is not to makes lists of observations and then turn them into poems. You don't even need to write down your three observations, though I think they'll keep better if you do. The point is to notice. Three observations. Then, possibly, three more, and three more, until you realize you're there.

There is a crack in everything,
That's how the light gets in.

—Leonard Cohen, singer-songwriter

18

the pain-body

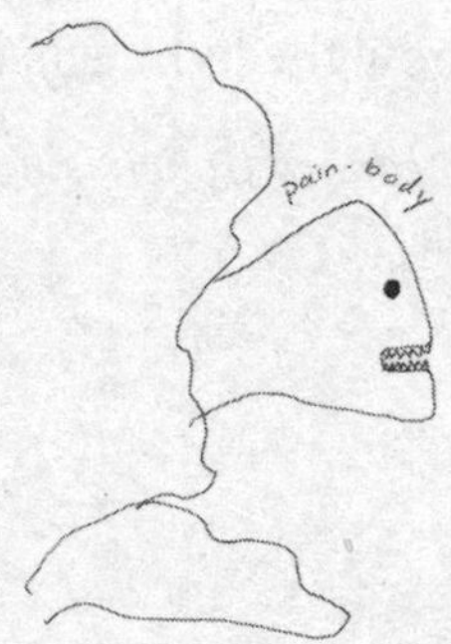

A friend recently gave me an audiobook version of *The Power of Now*. I listened to it for several weeks, in my car, and at the gym; I listened to some sections over and over. The author, Eckhart Tolle, had many insights to impart. They were—and are—the insights of every spiritual tradition: There is something beyond the material world, and we are a part of it; the body dies, but something survives and goes on; we must wake up to the present moment, which we lose by focusing on the past and future.

When I was nineteen, my friends and I read *Be Here Now* by Ram Dass. (In the sixties he was Richard Alpert, a Harvard professor who, along with Timothy Leary, experimented with the mind-expanding properties of LSD.) For my generation, he was one of the popularizers of those same spiritual teachings. He drew from the Tao Te Ching, the

Bhagavad-Gita, the Bible, the Koran—all the sacred texts. The same lessons find expression again and again.

One of the concepts in *The Power of Now* is the "pain-body," a negative energy field that can take us over, that feeds on our pain and wants our pain to continue and increase. Tolle says that the pain-body "will feed on any experience that resonates with its own kind of energy, anything that creates pain in whatever form."

The pain-body comes, first, from being born in a body. After that there are all the hurts and humiliations, large and small, which wound us. Everyone carries around pain from the past. We all know people who are in pain most of the time—Tolle would say they have very active pain-bodies. They're constantly down on themselves, or constantly medicating themselves with alcohol or drugs or entertainment. Whenever you ask how they are, they tell you their troubles. The message is always the same: I'm a basket case, I hurt, I'm overwhelmed, I'm misunderstood, I'm a victim. Nobody appreciates me. I'm ugly, I'm a bad person, I have no talent, I suck, I hate myself.

We've all been there. I know I have. My pain-body's pretty big.

Tolle suggests that we pay attention to our pain-body and recognize it, as a way to dissolve negativity. It's easy to be seduced by our own pain, to perversely enjoy the drama this creates.

Artists seem especially prone to believing that their pain makes them more interesting or more creative. Here's what I think: Art is a creative response to life. Pain and suffering are part of life, but they aren't all of it, and they shouldn't dominate us. We deeply want to be happy. The world is full of misery—philosopher Joseph Campbell called life "a horrific opera," which I think gets it just about right—but we have the responsibility not to create more misery, in the world or in ourselves. Many artists and spiritual teachers have encouraged the transcendence of pain, or transmutation of pain into joy.

Leo Tolstoy said, Add your light to the sum of light.

Jesus said, I am the Way, and the Truth, and the Light.

Rumi said, Become the light.

Johann Wolfgang von Goethe, on his deathbed, said: More light.

drawing your pain-body

This is one way to observe and work with the pain-body:

First do a short meditation. Close your eyes and imagine that your pain-body has a form. It might be anything: a tiger, a box, a volcano, a dead branch. Sit with your eyes closed and let an image arise, one that resonates with a feeling of pain or inadequacy or anger or despair. If nothing comes, wait. Let your frustration over not having an image give birth to one. Or so many may flood you that it's hard to choose one; feel your way into the image that has the most meaning for you, right now. Take slow, deep breaths, and let your mind quiet. The meditation can be only a few minutes, enough time for you to slow down and visualize.

The next step is to make that image concrete. Have handy an artist's pad, a few crayons or colored pencils or pens. Don't worry about the quality of your art—my drawing skills are those of a three-year-old. The important thing is to have a visual representation to work from.

Susan Browne and I used this exercise with a group of poets at Esalen, a retreat center in Big Sur, California. One woman pictured herself with logs in her chest and a wind passing through her, igniting the logs. Another drew a mean-looking pterodactyl with a big bony spine. "I like my pain," she said. "It makes me who I am." A third drew an eye in a box; several smaller eyes hung on hooks inside the box, while one enormous eye looked on as the box opened and closed. In another workshop, a man drew a figure with chains around his ankles, holding a hacksaw—like a jailed man holding a key. He understood how he had trapped himself. One writer saw herself encased in a thick spacesuit; another drew a tiny creature among giants; a third created a seductive spinning spider. Once I drew a drooping flower in a vase with no water (eerily, another woman in the group drew the same flower); another time I drew an egg with a wide crack, out of which peered a confused chick; at Esalen I drew an eel, with its long body trapped in a rock.

When I first read about the pain-body, I visualized mine as looking like Gollum, that J.R.R. Tolkien character who used to be a hobbit, but was now a pathetic, shrunken creature hissing *"Precioussss!"* as it schemed to reclaim the ring of Sauron. Soon afterward, I had an argument with the man I lived with, and my pain-body appeared as a snarling animal, intent on hurting someone I cared about. It was pure rage that time. Thinking about pain as a creature that morphs and shapeshifts helped me to recognize it and confront it more fully.

Once you've settled on an image that feels true to your pain-body at this moment, the next step is to write to it.

You can also write *as* your pain-body. Let it raise its weepy or savage little head and tell you about itself, or about you as it sees you. At Esalen, one woman created a dialogue between herself and her pain-body. Her poem was hilarious; she was able to make fun of her pain.

Since so much poetry seems to arise from pain, it's good to remember that everyone suffers. If you write only to display your pain, and believe it confers some special status, you're writing Vic Lit—Victim Literature. We all identify with our pain, often believing we *are* that person, the one who was hurt. You can spend your life stuck in past pain, reinforcing your sense of yourself as a victim.

If the purpose of poetry is to wake us up, then it can not only express pain, but point a way toward healing it.

pain pantoum

This is a way to play with form, providing a container for your pain-body poem. The exercise is also a way of revising, literally reseeing your material.

The pantoum is a fifteenth-century form from Malaysia that was later taken up by Western writers. It consists of four-line stanzas, or quatrains, as many as you need. Lines two and four of the first stanza become the first and third of the second stanza. Lines two and four of the second stanza become one and three in the third. You keep going like this until you're ready, or the poem is ready, to close.

For your last quatrain, lines one and three are already taken. That leaves two slots: lines two and four. Instead of writing new lines, go back to the beginning of your poem. The first line of your poem repeats as your last line. The third line of your poem repeats as line two in your last quatrain.

Sound confusing? Once you read a pantoum, the form is easy to see. Pantoums originally were metered and rhymed; many American versions only keep the principle of repeated lines.

Here's the poem I wrote originally when I visualized my pain-body as an eel (I'd seen one recently at the Monterey Aquarium). In this first version, I also used a rhyme scheme, *abcb:*

EEL

With your spike-teethed smile,
the length of you hidden,
tucked into your rock,
at the bottom of the ocean—

with your hole of an eye
that opens to nowhere,
with your hunger, your hunger,
and your eely despair—

Why do you call to me
from your glass case

Why do I read now
in your terrible face

something I had forgotten
until seeing you here,
alien, hideous,
holding me in your stare.

And here is my revision, in the form of a pantoum:

AQUARIUM EEL

With the length of you hidden
With your corrugated smile
Sheathed in your rock
In the hell of no ocean

With your corrugated smile
With your hole of an eye
In the hell of no ocean
That opens to nowhere

With your hole of an eye
With your hunger, your hunger
That opens to nowhere
With your eely despair

Your hunger, your hunger
Why do you call to me
With your eely despair
With your terrible face

Why do you call to me
Something I had forgotten
With your terrible face
Now you eel through me

Something I had forgotten
Sheathed in your rock
Now you eel through me
The length of you hidden

I had written my first poem in quatrains, with lines that were more or less self-contained. That made it easier to recast my lines in the form of a pantoum. (It's trickier if one line runs on to the next. If I'd written "with your hole / of an eye that opens," I would be struggling with transitions as I tried to fit in those repeated lines with the sense of the lines around them.) I also rethought and reordered some of my original language. With your own pantoum, you'll probably struggle with transitions from one line to the next, sometimes changing words in a line to make the poem succeed as a whole. As you move forward to write a line, you may need to back up to adjust a previous line. You don't need to repeat each line exactly, as I did; you can repeat or rearrange key words or phrases. "In the hell of no ocean," for example, might have been recast, in the repeated line, as "in your hellhole, the ocean," or "in your blue hell," or "deep in the ocean." The challenge and excitement of this form is fitting things together so the repetitions feel necessary and move the poem forward. I'm not sure my pantoum works completely, but I like it better than the original.

The pantoum has a terrific obsessive quality to it because of all the repetition. Try using it to transform other subject matter as well. Here are more pantoums to Google, so you can become familiar with the form:

"Evening Harmony," Charles Baudelaire
"Stillbirth," Laure-Anne Bosselaar
"Iva's Pantoum," Marilyn Hacker
"Parent's Pantoum," Carolyn Kizer
"Baby's Pantoum," Anne Waldman

19

ha! working with humor

If a man puts something in another man . . . It better be a bullet.

—*Bill Maher*

Humor is often suspect in poetry. Poetry is supposed to be serious business. I've been making some serious claims for poetry in this book—that it can heal, that it is an expression of self, that it is meant to wake us up. But when we are healed, we are happier. Our self-expression is creative. When we wake up to our lives we still have the pain, but we also get to experience the deep joy of being.

At least, that's what the spiritual teachers say. I'm not really there yet.

But the thing is, I believe them.

There's a difference between poems that rely on humor, and what I'll call Verse Lite. Verse Lite is—how shall I put this delicately?—facile and boring. It's one-dimensional when we want other levels—even while laughing. Especially while laughing.

Billy Collins, an often funny poet, said that humor is "not simply . . . a source of amusement, but . . . a way of seeing, a mode of perception." Humor is subversive. The absurdity of life set against life's incredible difficulty. A comic sensibility allows you to step back, to see the world ironically, to think clearly. It's something we value because it says, Lighten up. For a minute, play. Stop being politically correct. Question morals, question authority, question everything you've been taught.

Lenny Bruce said, "All my humor is based upon destruction and despair. If the whole world were tranquil, without disease and violence, I'd be standing on the breadline right in back of J. Edgar Hoover."

Some of the best comics go for the jugular. They look for the truth underneath the conventional. Bruce took on the morality and politics of his time, and skewered them. Good comics wade into uncomfortable territory, and then pull us in after them when we might want to stay safely onshore. Margaret Cho, addressing her Korean-American heritage, re-creates her mother's voice with its pidgin English. She jokes about racism, about body image, about the media pressure to conform. Jon Stewart's *The Daily Show* and Bill Maher's *Real Time* contain more "news of the world" than you'll find in network news. They have followed the disaster of Iraq, global warming, the dumbing down of journalism and America in general, gay marriage, political scandals, our eroding civil liberties.

But maybe I should lighten up here. I'm arguing for humor as a dissection tool, which it can be, though humor as delight, as pure play, is equally necessary. Lewis Carroll's "Jabberwocky" doesn't have any dark political intent—it's meant to be a nonsense poem—but it's great fun. Lucille Clifton has written a poem titled "to my last period"; the poem doesn't wring its hands over menopause, but whimsically captures a truth about women. Her "wishes for sons" has a slightly sharper edge:

WISHES FOR SONS

i wish them cramps.
i wish them a strange town
and the last tampon.
i wish them no 7-11.

i wish them one week early
and wearing a white skirt.
i wish them one week late.

later i wish them hot flashes
and clots like you
wouldn't believe. let the
flashes come when they
meet someone special.
let the clots come
when they want to.

let them think they have accepted
arrogance in the universe,
then bring them to gynecologists
not unlike themselves.

You've probably read poems that are too earnest, that plod along with their judgments, their righteous indignation, their persecuted narrators. You probably know people like this, too. If you're like me, you want to get away from them as quickly as possible. At least you want them to crack a smile once in a while.

In dire circumstances, humor may be the thing that saves you—which brings us to jokes.

chicken

Jokes and riddles are small universes of language. A joke is a story, or a moment, that depends on surprise—the punch line, the leap, a sudden shift in perception. A riddle can be pure metaphor: a question, a pause in which we search for an answer, and then the answer we didn't anticipate.

I wrote a poem called "Chicken" that begins, "Why did she cross the road?" You've probably heard many variations on the answer to this riddle. These are some amusing answers I found online:

> Albert Einstein: Whether the chicken crossed the road or the road crossed the chicken depends upon your frame of reference.
>
> Buddha: If you ask this question, you deny your own chicken-nature.
>
> Salvador Dalí: Fish.
>
> Darwin: It was the logical next step after coming down from the trees.
>
> Emily Dickinson: Because it could not stop for death.
>
> Ralph Waldo Emerson: It didn't cross the road; it transcended it.

My poem was about how we are trapped like chickens in cages, even when we think we are free. As with most of my poems, I didn't know where I'd go when I put down that first line. It's often best not to know where you're going. Try your own version of a poem that takes as its starting point the chicken riddle. Use the opening question to enter the chicken universe.

rewrites

Choose a joke or riddle with stock characters. A priest, a rabbi, and a nun. A farmer's daughter and a traveling salesman. Blondes. Lawyers. A politician/Jewish mother/liberal/therapist changing a lightbulb. Polacks. Italians. Irishmen. We're not talking about political correctness here. You might think about stereotypes and racial issues as you look up jokes and riddles online. Find a joke or riddle that speaks to you, and then create your own poem based on its characters.

I've always loved the riddle "How many Teamsters does it take to screw in a lightbulb?" "Thirty. Ya got a problem with that?" With that as a jumping-off point, I might go for the comedy of describing thirty hulking guys gathered in a small room under an empty light socket. Or I might take it in a serious direction and ask about Jimmy Hoffa, a former president of the Teamsters Union who disappeared under mysterious circumstances. You could use a blonde joke as a way to launch into feminist issues, or explore religion comically in a dialogue between a priest and a rabbi.

a poet walks into a bar

"A man walks into a bar . . ." That's the beginning of a joke with a lot of variations. Men, horses, skeletons, mushrooms, dogs, mice, and peanuts, in the universe of jokes, seem to require liquid refreshment. Go online and read some variations of "A —— walks into a bar." Then fill in the blank and write a poem in which something funny happens to your character.

high and low

"The Rape of the Lock," written in 1712, by Alexander Pope, is a parody of the traditional epic poem. The epic generally dealt with serious subjects—war, love, religious faith. Pope combined overblown language with the conventions of the epic—sacrifices to the gods, a journey to the underworld—for a less than epic subject. The "Rape" of the title refers to cutting a lock of a young woman's hair during a party. The humor arises from the gap between what's actually happening, and the form and language used to describe the "rape." Pope's intent was to satirize the trivial concerns of early eighteenth-century society.

Write a poem—it needn't be of epic length—in which you discuss something unimportant in a grandiose manner. For example:

> My lost sock is dying of loneliness. It can't bear another hour
> alone in its drawer. All around it the paired ones
> cuddle, and whisper to each other, and make plans
> for Saturday night. O sock! O single, unmated, white-
> patterned-with-yellow-ducks socks! Poor ducks,
> swimming alone through the dark drawer, pitifully quacking.

Well, you see how silly this can get.

a modest proposal

The tension between form and content offers a great opportunity for poets. In *A Modest Proposal*, another eighteenth-century satire, Jonathan Swift presented a detailed, reasoned argument suggesting a solution should poor Irish children become a burden to their parents: Just eat the little ones. The essay begins on a serious note, then deftly and gradually shifts gears, until we have these lines:

> I shall now therefore humbly propose my own thoughts, which I hope will not be liable to the least objection.
>
> I have been assured by a very knowing American of my acquaintance in London, that a young healthy child well nursed is at a year old a most delicious, nourishing and wholesome food, whether stewed, roasted, baked, or boiled, and I make no doubt that it will equally serve in a fricassee, or a ragout.

Swift's essay can be read in its entirety online. With that as a model, write a poem proposing a solution to some terrible or difficult problem: war, animal testing, racism. Be serious at first, and then shift to satire.

smile

Humor as a response to grief and pain is probably universal. People often share funny stories about a relative or friend after a funeral. The tension of an argument breaks when one of you cracks a joke. Timing is everything.

Sometimes humor is a diversion, keeping us from being overwhelmed by painful events.

Try to find a way to lighten a serious poem you've written with a touch of comedy. In almost every situation there is something humorous or absurd. Look at how Billy Collins writes about dead parents in "No Time":

> In a rush this weekday morning,
> I tap the horn as I speed past the cemetery
> where my parents are buried
> side by side beneath a slab of smooth granite.

Then, all day, I think of him rising up
to give me that look
of knowing disapproval
while my mother calmly tells him to lie back down.

⁂ 20

identity 2: race, class & privilege

My father was working-class. His father, who emigrated from Italy with his wife, had eleven children and was a butcher in New York City. My maternal grandmother was a single mother who supported her three children as a high school gym teacher. By the time my parents married, they had achieved much greater economic success than their parents.

I was raised in Bethesda, Maryland, in a neighborhood where the black maids stood on corners in the afternoons, waiting for the bus back to D.C. I went to good public schools. After leaving home, I earned a poverty-level income for many years. I was, as they say, "downwardly mobile," but I had the skills to survive, to make my way in the world, and I got them early in life.

Because I am a Caucasian-American in a culture that is predominantly white, I have blind spots. Sometimes I know what they are, and I can try to see them in a side mirror. But sometimes, I think, I don't even notice them. I can usually afford not to notice. This is the privilege of my skin color.

What does all this mean for my writing? It means I already have a whole boatload, so to speak, of cultural identities and assumptions. It means that those attitudes might be revealed in my writing, whether or not I'm aware of them.

Tony Hoagland observes that one's cultural attitudes can also be revealed by omission. In "Negative Capability: How to Talk Mean and Influence People," he writes:

> Why hasn't racial anxiety, shame and hatred—such a large presence in American life—been more a theme in poetry by Caucasian-Americans? The answer might be that Empathy is profoundly inadequate as a strategy to some subjects. To really get at the subject of race, chances are, is going to require some unattractive, tricky self-expression, something adequate to the paradoxical complexities of privilege, shame and resentment. To speak in a voice equal to reality in this case will mean the loss of observer-immunity-status, will mean admitting that one is not on the sidelines of our racial realities, but actually in the tangled middle of them, in very personal ways. Nobody is going to look good. Meanwhile, of course, American black poets have been putting the nasty topic on the table for a long time, in very personal ways.

Others who bring up the topic include Native American poets Sherman Alexie and Joy Harjo; Asian-American poets Jessica Hagedorn and Lawson Inada; and Latino poets Martin Espada and Sandra Cisneros. "In very personal ways" because, for these writers, the issue is undeniably personal, whereas if you're Caucasian-American, denial is often part of your conditioning.

Is it true, as Hoagland says, that empathy is "profoundly inadequate as a strategy"? I wonder. Fiction writers find their way into characters vastly different from themselves. Can't writers of poetry do the same? And if we use ourselves as characters, is it true that "nobody is going to look good" addressing the "nasty topic" of race? These are questions well worth considering.

There's a writing exercise about diction that I give my students. I ask them to think of charged, loaded words—button-pushing words—and to title their own poem with such a word or phrase. The poem needs to explore ways to complicate our feelings about the title. When I've done this in a classroom setting, I've asked for possible words and filled the blackboard with suggestions. This makes the air of the room very charged, and is instructive in and of itself. Look how powerful language can be! It's just a word, but put some of those words on the blackboard, or even in a book such as this, and you are inviting condemnation. Sex, race, and class: this is what the words revolve around.

America is supposed to be a classless society. But if you are poor, or working-class, you know better. Really, whatever your class, this is obvious if you are paying attention. There is language that defines your class, there are certain expectations and aspirations, there is a very real sense of separation from other people. The clothes you wear, the objects you accumulate, the car you drive, are all markers of class. A poor person can't relate to the kind of life pictured in a Pottery Barn or an L.L. Bean catalogue. Most immigrants to this country occupy the bottom rung of society. Meanwhile, the top 1 percent of the population holds about one-third of the wealth in the United States. A little over a third belongs to the next 9 percent. That leaves less than a third of the country's wealth for the remaining 90 percent.

There are, really, many Americas. It's just that most of them are often distorted, marginalized, or unacknowledged by the mainstream culture.

This poem by Gary Copeland Lilley shows us the flip side of the American dream: poverty, homelessness, violence. But there's tenderness, too, and a sense of hope, however fragile:

OUR LADY OF THE BIRDS

14th Street, the gentrified give a wide berth
to her prayers. Her dirt is offensive
and all the pigeons seem diseased.

She's old, the color of dust-covered patent leather,
layers of bad smelling clothes
hang off her thin body. Her gray hair is cut close.

At the House of Ruth, the shelter for women,
some sit outside with the bruises and a look I've seen
in my mother's kitchen. The stare of her marriage

before she put the knife in her husband's chest
and left him to drive himself to the hospital, ending
the beatings, after eighteen years of them.

He drove past woods and fields, the knife handle
in his peripheral vision, the blade cutting a little every time
he turned the wheel to Mercy.

Said he was lucky the blade missed his heart,
only thing that kept him from passing out and dying
beside the road was to focus on all those birds

flying past the windshield. Every afternoon
the old lady tosses seeds, the pigeons gather
at her different sized and colored shoes.

The bruised women watch from the yard
as the old lady raises her arms
and birds rise like prayers in her hands.

Here are some exercises that may help you approach "other Americas" or to consider race and class as they intersect with your own experiences.

1. Write about your relationship with your racial/cultural identity. When were you first aware of being Asian, Caucasian, Jewish, "different" from other people? Did you grow up within a certain group, and/or as an outsider to other groups? See if you can recall a specific incident when you experienced your "otherness."
2. Write about some of the messages you got about "other people," as a child—from parents, teachers, or other kids. Were "other people" better off, or worse off? Did you hear about people starving in Africa or Asia? Were "other people" supposedly lazier or better or greedier than you? Try to recall when these ideas were either confirmed—or overturned—through a specific encounter.
3. Write about a relationship you have, or had, with someone of a different race or class—a childhood friend, a lover, a coworker. Focus on a particular time when you were uncomfortable about your differences. Now think about a time when you found those differences enlightening or enlarging in some way. The poem might be about either of those times—or both of them.
4. Write a poem in which you describe in detail your envy of someone else's money or possessions.

5. Where did your parents originate? Your grandparents? Imagine you are one of your relatives from that place. This relative is thinking about the old ways of doing things and observing your life as it is now. Is that person approving, disapproving? What does that person want to tell you?
6. Write a poetic "résumé," describing several jobs you had. In each case, give us an image that helps us experience what the job was like for you.
7. Write a poem about the worst job you ever had.
8. Write about someone who does work you would never do.
9. Do you feel slightly ashamed of some possession because it cost so much money? Write a poem persuading a reader that you were totally justified in spending this much. Then write another poem in which you challenge your extravagance.
10. Go through a day without spending any money and write about how it feels.

⁂ 21

the whiskey on your breath: addictions

I don't need drugs. I am drugs.

—*Salvador Dalí*

We humans are an addictive species. Coffee every morning. A cigarette after a meal. Beer or wine or scotch at night, and sometimes a Bloody Mary for breakfast. William Faulkner had to drink first thing in the morning, just to get sober enough to function. Elizabeth Bishop, Charles Bukowski, Jack Kerouac, and a raft of other writers were alcoholics. Charles Baudelaire and Samuel Taylor Coleridge were addicted to opium. William Burroughs was a junkie. We become addicted to substances, to people, to behaviors. When I go into a hotel room and can't immediately get on the Internet to check my email, I'm anxious.

I found a web site that listed various addictions: to alcohol, bingeing, Coke (the soft drink), coke, coin collecting (watch out for those people), diuretics, excessive exercising, fame, joking about serious matters, kinky sex, masturbation, muscle relaxants, overachieving, people-pleasing, relationships, risky sports, Satanism, shock treatments, shopping, shoplifting, sleeping pills, TV, therapy (where do you get therapy for therapy addiction?), Valium, work. And that's just a partial list. I think we all must be addicted to something.

The web site www.addictionz.com says this: "All addictions block positive energy flow in the body."

Think about your own addictions—your obsessions, your vices, things you can't, or couldn't, live without. Anything that is blocking your life force, getting in your way. Addictions that might be killing you, like cigarettes and alcohol, or killing your relationship, like porn, or killing your anxiety, like Vicodin or Xanax or overwork. Things or people you're relying on a little too often. Maybe your habits and behavior are creating real problems in your life; or maybe you see them as benign. Needing a fix of reality TV is better than needing to score crack. But a steady diet of TV is probably as bad for your creativity as crack is for your body. When you think of certain behaviors this way—as blocking positive energy—some of them seem less benign. They begin to seem as if they might be in the way of something you want, like more happiness and peace of mind.

The title of this chapter refers to a poem by Theodore Roethke, "My Papa's Waltz." A boy is dancing in the kitchen with his drunk father. The boy loves his father's wild, rough dance, even when his father's belt buckle is scraping his cheek, even while his father beats time on his head. It's clear that the father has a problem, but it's equally clear that the boy loves his father. Maybe we're all ambivalent about addiction. There's a glamour and romance associated with addiction, especially with regard to artists. It makes for drama. To tell the truth of an addiction requires looking hard, at its appeal and also at its dark side. This excerpt from "Motel-by-the-Hour" by Nancy Pearson gives an unflinching account:

1.

I lost my straight shooter, a sawed-off sparkplug
somewhere in a cheap motel.
All night, I search for pipes—
tire gauge, rusted beer can, hollowed-out cigar.

Months ago, I drove across the country,
left my home in the wet hills of Tennessee,
found the unfolding pageant of billboards,
squashed possum, tugboat clouds,

hills repeating hills, freewheeling leaves going insane.
Thought I could drive my past away.
I'm here now and hunched over,
searching for a boost.

Behind me, that red suspension bridge
sinks into the deep fog,
leaves this bright world behind
for another.

2.

Strung out, Silva and I need a bump.
The wind, spring-loaded and snap-buckling
through the cypress, creeps in,
splinters the stash thin across the motel floor.

We are crawling and picking through the carpet.
Silva says, Stop pushing my head down, Reggie,

my knees got seeds mashed in them.
Night is a rerun re-run. Fight over a pebble high:

that long five minutes. Reggie watches us buck and kiss.
Silva on the floor again. (Stop pushing my head down, Reg.)
The shag hooks her silver hoop—
ear snagged and hanging off

like old fish bait. Stuck down there,
someone just cover her up.

Pearson's poem begins in the desperation of needing a high. Throughout the poem she presents us with opposites: getting high and being "stuck down there," the past and present, the "wet hills" of Tennessee and the "here" of cheap motels. The speaker is trapped in one world and unable to get to another. The erotic moment in the poem is unromantic, sordid. The damage, both physical and psychic, is vividly rendered.

Here are some suggestions for writing about addictions:

1. After making a list of your own addictions, tell the story of your most recent negative experience related to the addiction.
2. Write a love poem directly addressing one of your addictions, talking to it about what you get from it, in both positive and negative ways.
3. Write a poem in which you talk about every single thing, large or small, that you are addicted to in any way. From this, cull the most interesting language/addiction, and refocus your poem.
4. List the addictions of the people closest to you. Write about how these addictions have affected you. Describe scenes: your mother knocking back the scotch, your friend doing bong hits during reruns of *Weeds* (the HBO series about a suburban mother who

deals pot), imagining what your kid or partner does online for seven hours.

5. Recovery literature talks about your Addict, that part of you that wants to drink/smoke/behave badly. Your Addict can be seductive, or badger you, or rationalize a million reasons why you should just go ahead and give in. Write a poem in two voices, one that wants to overcome the addiction and the other that doesn't.
6. Give up a habit for forty-eight hours: wine, TV, your cell phone or email access. In your journal, keep a record of your craving. Write about how much you want it/him/her. See if there's an ebb and flow to your desire and your misery over not having what you want. Notice when the craving goes away (if it does), and how your mood changes. This might be a good exercise to do with a partner, so you have a "sponsor" to help you through. You can't do this exercise if you cheat; you really have to give something up.

   On the third day, see how you feel. Write about it.

III.

the poem's progress

My favorite thing is to go where
I've never been.

—*Diane Arbus, photographer*

⁂ 22

metaphor 1: the shimmer

In his *Poetics*, written in 350 B.C., Aristotle says, "The greatest thing by far is to have a command of metaphor. This alone cannot be imparted by another; it is the mark of genius, for to make good metaphors implies an eye for resemblances." Metaphor (from the Greek *metaphora*, "transference") speaks of one thing in terms of another, creating a kind of energy field, what I think of as "the shimmer": Blake's "To see a World in a Grain of Sand" gives us sand grain and world, simultaneously. (Simile does the same thing, only a bit more obviously: to say that a grain of sand is *like* a world would make the comparison explicit, and also change Blake's meaning.)

Every time we speak or write, we are drenched in metaphor. I said "drenched," but I might have used any number of verbs to describe the fact that language itself is metaphorical. We're steeped in metaphor, swimming in it, walking through its woods. I learned this from all those Greek and Latin roots that my mother found in the dictionary. The word "trivia," for example: from the Latin—*tri*, meaning three, *via*, meaning way or road. Where roads intersected, travelers would stop to talk and gossip before moving on. So the literal place they met, where the roads crossed, became an image for the kind of conversation that took place there. Now we don't think about three roads when we say that something is trivia. But the metaphor is there. Under the surface, buried.

We use these "dead" metaphors all the time without realizing it. One day, to say that someone sounds like a broken record may not remind anyone of albums or stereos. At that point, "broken record" will become a dead metaphor. People will forget about records, but the records will be in the language itself. Do you know where "mad as a hatter" comes from, or "going to hell in a handbasket"?

Even the word "record" is a metaphor for "round black pressed vinyl object." Someone coined (there's another metaphor) the term "record" because committing something to vinyl was like committing it to paper. The word "record" itself has this etymology: "Middle English, literally, to recall, from the Anglo-French *recorder,* from the Latin *recordari,* from *re-* + *cord-*, *cor* heart." So to know something "by heart" is to have it in your memory; and to know it by heart, again, is to have it in a recorded form. Every word is connected to other words, to history, to culture, to how we see.

The lake is a mirror. The guitar is a woman's body, the bird's song a squeaky door hinge, the raindrops tiny pushpins hitting the asphalt.

The essence of poetry: one thing in terms of another. And, crucially, one thing waking up another. Probably you're familiar with the image of a lake as a mirror. Probably it is no surprise to you that a guitar resembles a woman. But you might have perked up a little at the bird's song as a door hinge, or the raindrops as pushpins. Maybe you were encouraged, ever so slightly, toward closer attention.

Metaphor is perception; that's why it is so key to creativity. When we tell ourselves what we see, we can use language that dulls our awareness—"her eyes are dark pools"—or language that sharpens it: "My eyes, those girls that milk the light," a line by Attila Jozef.

The linguist George Lakoff wrote about the ways the language we use for concepts leads us to understand those concepts differently. The way we *talk about* something is also the way we *experience* it. One example he gives is this:

Argument is War.

How is an argument seen as war? Lakoff points out that we use phrases like *defending our position* or *marshaling our defenses.* We *win* or *lose* arguments. But what if argument were seen as a dance? Our language would reflect that, and what we mean by *argument* would change.

Again, we rarely notice that we are using metaphor when we say that we *defended our position.* This way of speaking is so familiar that the metaphor is effectively dead. This kind of metaphor is sometimes called dormant, or dying, because if we stop to think about it, we can see that a metaphor still exists.

The following exercises will help you toward that elusive "command of metaphor" that Aristotle admired.

waking the dead

Highlighting some figure of speech we usually pass over can bring it to life in interesting ways. Take the statement "The conversation died." The metaphor here, that we usually don't notice, is that a conversation is like a living creature. In the poem "Speck," Dean Young focuses on the word "died" and creates these lines:

> It's hard to keep the conversation alive
> but no one can find the do-not-resuscitate order.

You can imagine further turns on the dead or dying conversation:

The conversation developed terminal cancer.
The conversation fell into a coma.
The conversation lost its footing and went over a steep cliff.

Here's another example: "Love stinks." The implication is that love is something that decays, and smells bad: a rotting body; garbage; fumes. Playing with these ideas, you might arrive at the following:

Vultures have started circling our love.
The factories of love were poisoning the air.
I passed by a Dumpster full of love, and held my nose.

Below are more metaphors you can wake up; they're either dead, dying, or very tired. Start by trying to capture the equation; there may not be a single correlation. After you get the hang of this, start listing dead metaphors you come across, and experiment with them.

- A sudden fear gripped me.
- Night fell.
- The road snaked into the mountains.
- Music floated out an open window.
- Light spilled into the room.
- We hammered out our differences.
- The party was lethal until someone finally broke the ice.
- Our relationship was a dead end.
- He threw a tantrum.
- Her face fell.

My favorite recent example of a dead metaphor being jolted to life occurred while I was working on this chapter. A friend of mine, a criminal investigator, called to tell me about a case he had worked on. "The case had no legs," he said. "It was a double amputee crying out for prostheses." That, to my ears, was pure poetry.

waking up clichés

Clichés, while still recognizable as using metaphor or simile, are fatigued from too much use. That's why phrases like the ones below are going to bore readers and send them looking for something more interesting to do, like downloading music or watching somebody's cat on YouTube. Here are some popular clichés:

- My love is deeper than the ocean.
- I'm free as a bird.
- I'm trapped in the prison of my mind.
- There are walls around my heart.
- I cried a river of tears.
- I traveled along the road of life, a lonely wanderer . . .
- The wind whispered in the trees.
- Her face lit up.
- You are my sunshine.

Clichés are more than tired phrases. As George Lakoff points out, our entire *way of thinking* may be so familiar we aren't aware of it. There are clichés of thought, clichéd images, clichéd moves you can make in any poem. The cliché is the overused, the unexamined way to say something that is usually much more complex.

Life is complicated. Clichés fail because they don't reflect truth. They're easy, and so they lie. As you've seen, poets lie in many ways, but good poets don't mess with life's complexity.

The revisions of "The conversation died" and "Love stinks" are more detailed and specific than the original. That's key. You can often rescue a cliché by making it specific. For example, "the road of life" is a pretty tired image. But read C. P. Cavafy's "Ithaca," which opens, "When you set out on your journey to Ithaca, / pray that the road is long." Cavafy explores truth that cliché can't capture. How does he do it? He makes the road of life the road to Ithaca, gives it all the texture and resonance of a myth—the Greek hero Odysseus returning home—and creates a moving poem about "the journey of life."

Here are some examples of waking up clichés:

I'm free as a bird.

From the sky, the troubled world looks smaller.
My oiled wings, my muscles, my hollow bones—
I hardly feel them, they carry me so lightly.

I cried a river of tears.

When you left I cried the Ganges, I cried the Amazon, I cried the entire Mississippi.
I cried the Monongahela, polluted with chemical runoff and old condoms.
I cried until the levees broke and the city of my heart was ruined.

In the examples above, I didn't need to make the comparison obvious and explicit. This is good to notice in the poems you read—how a poet makes one thing into another and we recognize what is happening without needing to be told.

rolling your own

The right simile or metaphor can nail a description in a way nothing else can. Call up a second thing in our mind's eye (or ear), and the first comes clear. In a harsh poem about a boy killing a dog and throwing it over a falls, Toi Derricote describes the decomposing body that finally "lay on the bottom like a scraggly rug." There it is, unforgettably, thanks to her simile.

Carry your journal with you for one day and note not only the physical objects you see, but also what they resemble. As your model, you can use the famous two-line poem by Ezra Pound, "In a Station of the Metro," which compares the faces the poet sees to flower petals. Here are three examples, taken down in the room where I am writing this chapter:

> Row of pans hanging from kitchen hooks:
> ducks strung feetfirst in a Chinese market.
>
> The clock keeps clicking,
> an obsessive conductor tapping a baton.
>
> Laughter from the house next door:
> horses whinnying in the field while I stand in my stall.

change the follow-through

Look at what is happening in these metaphors from poet Jeffrey McDaniel:

> I went into the bar and ordered a childhood dream.
> ("The Wounded Chandelier")

There's a field where I grow only bruises,
inner gnawing, and heartache.
("The Farmer")

I'll see your cross-eyed pigeon
and raise you a jar of epileptic brains.
("Opposites Attack")

Where we expect one thing—a literal drink, a crop, a card game—we receive a metaphorical surprise. Try this technique by starting out with a concrete description—for example, "I shelved my books alphabetically." Then substitute a surprise for the obvious. It might be abstract or concrete. "I shelved my humiliations alphabetically." "I shelved my lovers alphabetically." "I shelved my nightmares alphabetically."

Another example: "She put her packages on the table" might become "She put her heart on the table." "She put her indifference on the table." "She put her lies on the table." Try out several concrete sentences and substitutions. Let one of them lead you further into the shimmer of metaphor.

23

white heat, necessary coldness

> Dare you see a soul at the White Heat?
>
> —*Emily Dickinson*

When I wrote poems in high school, they were all about my feelings. In my late twenties, when I began seriously reading poetry and trying to write it, I realized that pouring out my desire or sadness or loneliness was not enough. As satisfying as it was to write in my journal, I could see that something besides deep feeling was required. I needed craft.

Beginning writers tend to think that craft is their enemy. As long as they believe that, they will remain beginners, no matter how many years they write. When I attend harmonica workshops—which are something like writers' conferences, only louder—our instructors, all accomplished musicians, talk about the feeling. But mostly they talk about technique. Professional musicians are all about tone production, scales, harmonies, rhythmic structures. Writers are all about the sentence, the fragment, the period, the verb, the line break. The associations words make, their sounds in the mouth, the tone and pacing and structure of a piece, the unfolding of narrative or idea or repetition. All of those, all at once, and more.

One technique you can use to handle emotion on the page is to "write it colder." This is from a letter written by Anton Chekhov, the great Russian playwright and short story writer:

> When you want to make the reader feel pity, try to be somewhat colder—that seems to give a kind of background to another's grief, against which it stands out more clearly. Whereas in your story the characters cry and you sigh. Yes, be more cold . . . The more objective you are, the stronger will be the impression you make.

I often stress the importance of "coldness" with my students. It's easy to make the mistake of overwriting—breaking out the violins to play schmaltzy music. Trying to be dramatic, you may become melodramatic. On the other hand, you may pull back so far that the reader has no idea why he or she should care. Finding the balance takes time. It's like any social interaction: we step back from people who are too pushy, who want to tell us what to think or how to feel. But if we get no energy from them, we don't even want to know them.

How can you balance the two poles, and craft poems that are full of feeling without being sentimental, that are rich with idea as well as emotion? The following poems succeed at striking this balance, and can show you some techniques for your own work.

imagery

BAG OF MICE

I dreamt your suicide note
was scrawled in pencil on a brown paperbag,

& in the bag were six baby mice. The bag
opened into darkness,
smoldering
from the top down. The mice,
huddled at the bottom, scurried the bag
across a shorn field. I stood over it
& as the burning reached each carbon letter
of what you'd written
your voice released into the night
like a song, & the mice
grew wilder.

—*Nick Flynn*

In "Bag of Mice," a son is remembering a mother's suicide (it's clear when you read Flynn's book *Some Ether*). He doesn't "cry and sigh" like the characters Chekhov mentions. The poem is precise, self-observant, and particular in its descriptions. Flynn focuses on the surreal dream-image of baby mice in a paper bag that is smoldering, slowly burning, while the speaker stands and watches. The note, "scrawled in pencil" so that it seems temporary already, begins disappearing as the bag burns down toward the mice. The speaker stands over the bag but doesn't act. He seems as helpless as the mice, unable to stop this terrible thing from happening. All he can see, as he looks into the bag, is darkness. The darkness of the mother's reasons? The darkness of grief? The mother seems released, by the close of the poem, but the mice—and by implication, the son—are not.

The bag in this poem is symbolic, metaphorical. The poet doesn't try to stun us with the awful details of the suicide. That event occurs "offstage," so to speak, and haunts the poem as the drama of the mice unfolds. This is one way to achieve "coldness." Capturing the complexity of emotion through imagery is what makes this poem successful—and moving.

restraint

THE DEATH OF THE BALL TURRET GUNNER

From my mother's sleep I fell into the State,
And I hunched in its belly till my wet fur froze.
Six miles from earth, loosed from its dream of life,
I woke to black flak and the nightmare fighters.
When I died they washed me out of the turret with a hose.

—*Randall Jarrell*

"A ball turret was a Plexiglas sphere set into the belly of a B-17 or B-24, and inhabited by two .50 caliber machine-guns and one man, a short small man. When this gunner tracked with his machine-guns a fighter attacking his bomber from below, he revolved with the turret; hunched upside-down in his little sphere, he looked like the fetus in the womb. The fighters which attacked him were armed with cannon firing explosive shells. The hose was a steam hose." (Jarrell's note)

This poem about a World War II gunner delivers an emotional knockout in just five lines. Maybe the emotion one feels, after reading it, could be described as shock that gives way to something else—grief, anger, pity. The brief life of the gunner—he hardly has a life, moving quickly from being born in the first line, to his military service in the second, to suddenly waking "six miles from earth" (a reference to being six feet under, one of many reversals in the poem) in lines three and four, to his unceremonious death in line five. Born in order to go to war and die, this dead airman seems to be the only one even to witness his fate. Yet the tone is never overwrought—the power here comes from so much that is held back.

A prose poem by Carolyn Forché, "The Colonel," achieves its power in a similar way. The speaker delivers terrible information in a matter-of-fact, almost reportorial manner that allows us to feel the emotion. In that poem, set in the 1980s during the civil war in El Salvador, a colonel dumps a jar of human ears on the dinner table. It's a scene that might only be horrific or grotesque, except for the way the poet tells us about those ears. The poem ends: "Some of the ears on the floor / caught this scrap of his voice. Some of the ears on / the floor were pressed to the ground."

Here's my rewrite of Jarrell's poem to show you how badly his material could have been handled:

I was ripped from my mother's womb, like a chimp stolen by poachers
and carried in a cage, crying for its mother, and put into a cold zoo.
I was moaning and frozen. I awakened to a chilling nightmare.
When I died my bloody death, blasted to pieces, they took a hose
and washed me out of the turret, onto the cold, cold ground.

My version, first of all, is tone-deaf. "Ripped from my mother's womb" tries to tug at the heartstrings, and to make things worse, there's the baby chimp crying for *its* mother. Next there's the overblown cliché of "a chilling nightmare," the unnecessary "my bloody death" and the further unwelcome detail of being "blasted to pieces" (something we understand in the Jarrell poem without needing to have it spelled out). The "cold, cold ground" again tries too hard to make us feel something.

Listen, too, to the powerful music in Jarrell's poem, which also helps deliver the emotion.

hyperbole, humor, irony

THE GOOD KISS

And then there was the night, not long
After my wife had left me and taken on the world-
Destroying fact of a lover, and the city
Roared in flames with it outside my window,
I brought home a nice woman who had listened
To me chant my epic woe for three

Consecutive nights of epic drinking,
Both of us holding on to the bar's
Darkly flowing river of swirling grain
As my own misery flowed past and joined
The tributary of hers, our murmured consolations
Entwining in precisely the same
Recitative, the same duet that has beyond
All doubt been sung in dark caves
Of drink since the very beginning
Of despair, the song going on until there was nothing
For it but to drive through an early summer
Thunderstorm in the windy night
To my little East Side apartment and gently
Take off her clothes and lay her down
On my bed by the light
Of a single candle and the lightning
And kiss her for a long time in gratitude
And then desire, and then gently kiss the full
Moons of her breasts, which I discovered
By candlelight were not hers, exactly;
Under each of them was the saddest,
Tenderest little smile of a scar,
Like two sad smiles of apology.
I had them done
So he wouldn't leave, she said,
But in the end he left anyway, her breasts
Standing like two cold cathedrals
In the light of the flaming city
And I kissed the little wounds
He had left her, as if I could heal them
And kissed the nipples he had left behind
Until they smoldered like the ashes

Of a campfire the posse finds
Days after the fugitive has slept there
And moved on, drawn by the beautiful
And terrible light of the distant city.

—George Bilgere

Bilgere's poem achieves some of its necessary "coldness" through exaggeration and humor. If "less is more"—if understatement and matter-of-factness are one way to counter melodrama—it's also true that more, used in the right way, can be very effective. If a poet writes, "My lover left me and it destroyed my world," we may feel sympathetic and understand, but at the same time we pull back and say, "Wait a minute. That's a bit much, however awful it was." But Bilgere doesn't say it earnestly. By taking the image to absurd lengths, he makes it humorous. Not only is the man's world destroyed, but "the city / roared in flames with it outside my window." The speaker goes on this way, acknowledging his pain but also mocking himself—his "epic woe" and "epic drinking," his misery described as a river that flows from the swirls of wood grain in the bar. The river of the couple's shared misery then becomes music, and again the images are ramped up for comic effect: the "dark caves / Of drink," "the very beginnings / Of despair." And just when we think the writer is going to ruin the poem with sentimentality—a candle is lit, lightning flashes, her breasts are "full moons"—he surprises us. It's that surprise, both funny and sad, that moves us into emotional involvement. The encounter isn't romanticized, yet we care about these lovers.

form

Dorothy Parker often used wit and irony as a way of countering/delivering emotional content. Read her poem "Résumé"—a metered and rhymed little ditty on various ways to kill yourself. The form itself contributes to the humor and the tension. Form also works this way in Philip Larkin's "This Be the Verse," which opens, "They fuck you up, your mum and dad," and closes by suggesting that we exit life quickly and not have any children. The lilt of the meter is in marked contrast to the speaker's dark thoughts—a contrast that creates the necessary space for us to consider the emotion.

Contemporary poet Molly Peacock, who often writes in traditional forms, said, "I feel the initial choice, the conscious choice, of one traditional verse form over another, is not always the choice to match the feeling, but rather a choice to contain, to control, or otherwise make the feeling safe to explore." Working within the constraints of a form, you may paradoxically be freed to release strong emotions. See how form works in this sonnet by Elizabeth Barrett Browning:

GRIEF

I tell you, hopeless grief is passionless;
That only men incredulous of despair,
Half-taught in anguish, through the midnight air
Beat upward to God's throne in loud access
Of shrieking and reproach. Full desertness,
In souls as countries, lieth silent-bare
Under the blanching, vertical eye-glare
Of the absolute Heavens. Deep-hearted man, express
Grief for thy Dead in silence like to death—
Most like a monumental statue set
In everlasting watch and moveless woe
Till itself crumble to the dust beneath.
Touch it; the marble eyelids are not wet:
If it could weep, it could arise and go.

Browning's poem insists that "hopeless grief is passionless." If you are still crying out, cursing God or fate, you're only "half-taught in anguish." When you plumb the absolute depths of grief, the poet says, you reach a barren, silent landscape. Not "God's throne," where there might be someone to cry out to, but "the blanching, vertical eye-glare / Of the absolute Heavens." How grim that sounds—devoid of anything remotely human or consoling. Then we arrive at another image—the statue, which stands in "moveless woe." "Moveless" works literally with the concept of a statue—a statue doesn't move. But the woe, the sorrow, isn't moving either. It's as if the sorrow is fixed there. I also think of "moveless" as in "unmoved"—clearly the statue is "moved" in the sense that it represents grief, but at the same time, it *can't move.* It's trapped, frozen. "If it could weep, it could arise and go." We could leave behind a lesser grief. But if we are "deep-hearted," Browning says, we have to bear the awful, essential truth of loss.

So why a sonnet to convey this? A sonnet is concise. It has to be, at only fourteen lines. That puts a certain pressure on language and situation. In addition, a sonnet has certain fixities: the fourteen lines; the length of those lines (roughly ten syllables); the rhythm (iambic pentameter—da-DUM-da-DUM-da-DUM-da-DUM-da-DUM is the underlying beat you should hear); a rhyme scheme (in this case *abba, abba, cde, cde*—look at the words at the ends of the lines and you'll see the pattern). Traditionally, a sonnet also has a "turn," or *volta*, after the eighth line, signaling a shift from what has been laid out. In this sonnet, the *volta* occurs with "Deep-hearted man . . ."—slightly early. Browning moves from telling us about those whose grief isn't hopeless, to advising us to experience its silent, profound, and essential depths. The Italian sonnet form she uses here requires the writer to set out an idea or situation in eight lines, to expand or deepen that in the next six, and to come to conclusion by the end of line fourteen. The strictness of the form controls the emotion, yet also allows it.

a series of exercises

Present emotion. Make a list of the emotional situations that are powerful for you right now. Are you in love? Falling out of love? Are you grieving for something or someone? Are you angry at your friend, your mother, a political figure? Maybe you're happy for no apparent reason, or depressed without knowing why. After you've listed a few things that are affecting you, choose one and free-write for ten minutes about your feelings and the situation creating them. Now you've got your raw material. Take that material through the following transformations:

1. Find a metaphor that captures the emotion. This can be difficult, if a metaphor hasn't shown up naturally in the free-write. It helps to start with a simile: "Falling in love with you is like . . ." "Losing my brother feels like . . ." "My anger, if it had a shape, would look like . . ." Once you can get to what the feeling is like, abandon "like."
2. Version two: Condense the experience to a few lines—no more than ten. Use short, matter-of-fact sentences. (Don't worry about the metaphor in #1. You may want to abandon that and try something new. The main thing is to focus on tone and condensation.)
3. Change the emotional tone; use wildly extravagant exaggeration for comic effect, as Bilgere does in "The Good Kiss."
4. Bring a formal principle into play: rhymed couplets, ten-syllable lines, anything that imposes rules on your material. Try an acrostic, as Anne Waldman does in "He Who Once Was My Brother"; or an abecedarium, beginning each successive word or line or stanza with successive letters of the alphabet.

Past emotion. Make a list of past emotional situations. After free-writing on one or more, take your material through the same transformations as for present emotion.

For at least one of these situations, you may find that you no longer have that much emotion invested in something you once felt strongly about. This is an interesting subject for a poem. Write about it; your poem could be serious or witty or nostalgic or ironic—whatever comes to mind.

"We Feel Fine." The web site www.wefeelfine.org was created by Jonathan Harris and Sep Kanvar as "an exploration of human emotion on a global scale." The site searches blogs all over the world for the phrases "I feel . . ." and "I am feeling . . ." and creates a database of human emotion in various forms: a swirling nebula of particles, lists of "I feel . . ." statements, images, and much more. Especially fascinating are the montages: "I feel . . ." statements paired with images and posted on the site. Spend some time there. You might want to do your own post, on the page or in cyberspace.

Pleasures. Write some short prose poems that try to capture small moments of joy from both the past and present rather than focus on highly dramatic emotional moments. Here are two prose poems from *Pleasure*, by Gary Young.

> It's a joy to be subtracted from the world. Holding my son's naked body against my own, all I feel is what he is. I cannot feel my own skin. I cannot feel myself touching him, but I can recognize his hair, the heft of his body, his warmth, his weight. I cannot measure my own being, my subtle boundaries, but I know my son's arms, the drape of his legs, smooth and warm in a shape I can measure. I have become such a fine thing, the resting-place for a body I know.

*

> When I was a young man and found I had cancer, my friends held a benefit. There was music and dancing, and when the night was over, they gave me a paper bag filled with cash. My wife then was always

worried about money, but whenever she panicked, I reached into
the sack and handed her a fistful of bills. I'll never be that rich again.
Not a moment escaped me. I had everything I needed and nothing to
lose. I've never been happier than when I was dying.

Young's first poem is one of quiet happiness, the simple pleasure of a father holding his son. In the second, there is the drama and tension of the cancer—set against the realization that each moment is precious. That insight is enough. It is, in fact, everything.

✳ 24

a bag of tricks

Here are a few tricks to help you in writing or revising your drafts. The more comfortable you become with each of them, the easier it will be to pull one out when you need it.

1. Put your adjectives after your nouns.

> I saw the best minds of my generation destroyed by madness,
> starving hysterical naked . . .
>
> —*Allen Ginsberg, "Howl"*

> The tiger,
> marvellously striped and irritable, leaps
>
> —*Frank O'Hara, "Chez Jane"*

2. Delay the subject of your sentence. This is an especially useful way to open a poem, to create tension right away at the level of syntax.

> Because I could not stop for Death—
> He kindly stopped for me—
>
> —*Emily Dickinson, 712*

> Stiff in our black funeral ties and jackets,
> my brother and I crept out the kitchen door,
>
> —*Richard Newman, "Grampa's Liquor Bottles"*

> Leaping out of the barn dance of my brain, where everyone else
> can hip-hop, enjoy their murky drinks laced with Ecstasy,
> and because that cute blonde in the corner with the shirtless guy,
> dancing like she wants to smear the tattoos off his chest with her tits,
> could be my daughter, I dash off to a middle-ageish bar,
>
> —*Barbara Ras, "Where I Go When I'm Out of My Mind"*

> When I have fears that I may cease to be
> Before my pen has gleaned my teeming brain,
> Before high-pilèd books, in charact'ry,
> Hold like rich garners the full-ripened grain;
> When I behold, upon the night's starred face,
> Huge cloudy symbols of a high romance,
> And think that I may never live to trace
> Their shadows, with the magic hand of chance;
> And when I feel, fair creature of an hour,
> That I shall never look upon thee more,
> Never have relish in the faery power

Of unreflecting love!—then on the shore
Of the wide world I stand alone, and think
Till Love and Fame to nothingness do sink.

—*John Keats, "When I Have Fears"*

3. An interruption: Put something between your subject and your verb.

The just-fledged baby owl a waiter has captured under a tree
 near the island restaurant
seems strangely unfazed to be on display on a formica table,

—*C. K. Williams, "Owl"*

And what rough beast, its hour come round at last,
Slouches towards Bethlehem to be born?

—*William Butler Yeats, "The Second Coming"*

4. Another interruption: Use dashes or parentheses.

the art of losing's not too hard to master
though it may look like (*Write* it!) like disaster.

—*Elizabeth Bishop, "One Art"*

5. Start with a pronoun and then give us the noun it refers to.

What do they sing, the last birds
Coasting down the twilight,

—*Galway Kinnell, "Last Songs"*

I've tried to seal it in,
that cross-grained knot

—*Stanley Kunitz, "The Knot"*

6. Double or triple your subject, but use one verb.

    The snows of the Tyrol, the clear beer of Vienna
    Are not very pure or true.

—Sylvia Plath, "Daddy"

    My methedrines, my double-sun,
    Will give you two lives in your one,

—Thom Gunn, "Street Song"

7. Near the end of a free-verse poem, find a place to create a rhyme with your last word.

    I, with no rights in this matter,
    Neither father nor lover.

—Theodore Roethke, "Elegy for Jane"

    to work his mojo he lick my pearl to
    feel it glow. makes my hair grow

—Wanda Coleman, "Chuck Man"

8. Close a free-verse poem with a metrical line, especially one in iambic pentameter.

9. Repeat a word or phrase near the end of a poem, for greater intensity.

    What did I know, what did I know
    of love's austere and lonely offices.

—Robert Hayden, "Those Winter Sundays"

until everything
was rainbow, rainbow, rainbow!
And I let the fish go.

—Elizabeth Bishop, "The Fish"

10. Combine one or more of the above strategies in a single sentence:

MacDonagh and MacBride
And Connolly and Pearse
Now and in time to be,
Wherever green is worn,
Are changed, changed utterly:
A terrible beauty is born.

—William Butler Yeats, "Easter 1916"

The strategies Yeats uses here: multiple subjects with a single verb; an interruption between the subjects and the verb; a repeated phrase for added intensity; and a rhyme with the poem's last word (actually a part of the rhyme scheme of the entire poem, so that each stanza, as well, has a feeling of finality).

25

the poem's progress

> Without Contraries is no Progression.
>
> —*William Blake*

The way each poem unfolds, from beginning to end, is unique. Every poem you read or write has to move us from where we started to a place we didn't know we were going. If a poem goes nowhere, it's dead. Many poems fail in this manner: they set something up, and then nothing happens. The writer relates a series of events but doesn't know what to make of them. Or describes an emotional moment and can't deepen it, explore it, lean on it until it gives way. This is the problem Sylvia Plath was describing when she wrote in frustration of some of her poems, "They are not pigs or fish, though they have a piggy and a fishy air." She couldn't make them live.

There is no way to teach that mysterious, elusive thing that breathes life into a poem, that gives it, literally, inspiration. It's essential that you have something at stake, some urgency or deep inner need. The poem doesn't have to be an elegy for your mother or a meditation on despair; your deep need might be playful or joyous, or involve the working out of a philosophical idea. But if you aren't passionate about your poem, chances are a reader won't be either.

That passion should extend to everything in the poem. Its language, of course. Its syntax, lines, imagery, statements, sounds, rhythms, levels of thinking and imagination. And its progression, by which I mean its structure—how you shape the whole of the poem, an intricate mixture of all the things I just mentioned. And more.

If this sounds elusive, that's because it is. By studying how other writers have found their way through poems, you'll come closer to understanding how to shape your own. Also, you'll gain distance from your own work—that "necessary coldness" Chekhov talked about. This is important, especially if you are very close to your material: writing a heartbroken poem about a lover who has just left you, or expressing anger at a government sending kids to war and cutting social programs. If you want to make poetry out of these subjects, you have to step back.

three sonnets

A traditional form like the sonnet offers ways to progress through a poem. Lay out your opening idea in the first eight lines, deepen or amplify it for the next six. If it's a Shakespearean sonnet, the closing couplet can deliver a kicker. But two sonnets may have very different ways of progressing. Go back and reread "Grief" by Elizabeth Barrett Browning, on page 194. The sonnet opens with the statement "I tell you, hopeless grief is passionless." Essentially, it opens with a thesis. Browning is making an argument, developing it, "proving" it. By the end she's given us the image of that statue, and it's hard to argue with a poem that asks us to trust the evidence of our own senses:

Touch it; the marble eyelids are not wet:
If it could weep, it could arise and go.

The poet makes a wonderful move here. In our imagination, we touch the statue and have to agree with her: A statue can't cry. So we have to acknowledge as well the truth of her final line, that leap to the possibility—or impossibility—of the statue walking away, the impossibility of escape from the grief the poem describes.

Now look at this contemporary sonnet by Lucia Perillo:

THE BODY MUTINIES

When the doctor runs out of words and still
I won't leave, he latches my shoulder and
steers me out doors. Where I see his blurred hand,
through the milk glass, flapping good-bye like a sail
(& me not griefstruck yet but still amazed: how
words and names—medicine's blunt instruments—
undid me. And the seconds, the half seconds,
it took for him to say those words). For now,
I'll just stand in the courtyard watching bodies
struggle in then out of one lean shadow
a tall fir lays across the wet flagstones.
Before the sun clears the valance of gray trees
and finds the surgical-supply-shop window
and makes the dusty bedpans glint like coins.

Browning and Perillo have both used the form of the Italian sonnet (whose rhyme scheme is abba, abba, cde, cde). But where Browning opens with a statement, Perillo begins *in media res*, in the middle of things: a woman who's just been given bad news in a doctor's office. For the first eight lines, we're with the stunned speaker as the doctor "steers" her (she can't seem to move of her own accord yet) outside. He "latches" her shoulder—you can see the gesture, the doctor putting his arm around her, but Perillo doesn't say "latches on." "Latches," as a verb, is usually applied to a door or window, something that opens and closes. This is a threshold moment, the door of illness suddenly opening, the door of health slamming shut. The sight of the doctor's "blurred hand, / through the milk glass" reinforces that awareness. After this moment of physical transition, we hear about the emotional one: the speaker, "not grief-struck yet but still amazed" by the speed of the transition. At the end of line eight is the poem's turn, or *volta:* "For now," while the woman stands there still trying to take in whatever terrible news has just been delivered. The scene comes to us through this woman's eyes. She doesn't see people, but "bodies." They're struggling in and out of a shadow, which might represent death, the sense of a shadow laid over a life.

The last three lines contain another shift, as the sun is about to clear "the valance of gray trees." Valance suggests a window again, before we get to the physical "surgical-supply-shop window." The speaker is in that hyperaware state where everything takes on an awful clarity. In Greek mythology, coins were placed on the eyes of the dead as payment to Charon, who ferried souls across the river Styx into the underworld. The poem ends poised between life and death.

How differently Perillo's sonnet progresses from Browning's, which has moved from thesis statement to examples to addressing us directly and inviting our participation. The sonnet form suggested ways of proceeding, but the two poems don't proceed in the same way. And neither proceeds like this sonnet by Shakespeare:

SONNET 130

My mistress' eyes are nothing like the sun;
Coral is far more red, than her lips' red:
If snow be white, why then her breasts are dun;

If hairs be wires, black wires grow on her head.
I have seen roses damasked, red and white,
But no such roses see I in her cheeks;
And in some perfumes is there more delight
Than in the breath that from my mistress reeks.
I love to hear her speak, yet well I know
That music hath a far more pleasing sound;
I grant I never saw a goddess go,
My mistress, when she walks, treads on the ground:
  And yet, by heaven, I think my love as rare,
  As any she belied with false compare.

At first this speaker seems highly critical of his mistress. She has "black wires" on her head, her breath "reeks." But as the ending makes clear, Shakespeare is mocking the overblown romantic comparisons other poets (and he himself, in some of his earlier poems) use to describe their lovers. The first twelve lines of the poem are structured as a series of conventional images for beauty, followed by the poet's corrections, his insistence on fidelity to the real. He refuses those inaccurate images—what he calls "false compare." His mistress isn't a goddess, but a woman. "I grant I never saw a goddess go," he says wryly. "My mistress, when she walks, treads on the ground." The last two lines are what upend the poem and make clear its whole meaning. It's significant that Shakespeare goes from "the ground" to the phrase "by heaven," signaling us that his love is praiseworthy.

Three sonnets: same form, different structure.

further complexity

BLANDEUR

If it please God,
let less happen.
Even out Earth's
rondure, flatten
Eiger, blanden
the Grand Canyon.
Make valleys
slightly higher,
widen fissures
to arable land,
remand your
terrible glaciers
and silence
their calving,
halving or doubling
all geographical features
toward the mean.
Unlean against our hearts.
Withdraw your grandeur
from these parts.

—*Kay Ryan*

The first striking thing about this poem is its title, "Blandeur"—an invented word. If you know Gerard Manley Hopkins's poem "God's Grandeur," you can see where Ryan's poem comes from. Hopkins's poem begins, "The world is charged with the grandeur of God." The speaker in Ryan's poem doesn't disagree with this. But whereas Hopkins begins with a factual statement of his belief, Ryan begins with a kind of prayer. "Let less happen." The entire poem basically restates that request, specifically or generally. So how does the poem manage to progress, to move somewhere, if it's simply asking the same thing in different ways? Through the pure intensity of asking for less to happen. "Less happening" means, for this speaker, that the entire world needs to change radically. The speaker is not just asking for a little peace and quiet. The poem's intensity builds from those first two lines, asking that God remake the earth, undoing his own creation. The adjective "terrible" also deepens the sense of urgency. I love it that by this time the speaker doesn't care if the world's "geographical features" are halved or doubled—as long as they stop, are silent. And then the direct, and to me very moving, line: "Unlean against our hearts"—the revelation of the reason *why* the speaker wants less to happen, wants the world to be so different. It's like saying, "Give me Prozac! I feel too much." The enormity of life is overwhelming. It takes us up, then sends us plummeting down. God's grandeur turns out to be less positive than in the Hopkins poem. Read "God's Grandeur"—also a sonnet—and you'll see a different vision, one that inspired Ryan to express her own.

Another strength of Ryan's poem: the sounds. All of her poems are a pleasure to read for their tight weave of rhymes. Listen to how much is going on in such a short time:

> happen flatten blanden Canyon
> even Earth Eiger
> slightly higher widen
> higher fissures arable terrible
> land remand
> calving halving doubling
> features mean unlean
> hearts parts

And there's that trick I mentioned earlier: putting a word near the end of the poem that rhymes with the final word. So we have a sense of closure when "hearts" calls out and the last word of the poem, "parts," answers.

Elizabeth Bishop's poem "The Fish" begins, "I caught a tremendous fish." More than seventy lines later, the poem ends, "And I let the fish go." On one level, nothing happens. Bishop creates movement by closely considering that fish, right down to "the pink swim-bladder / like a big peony." By the end of the poem, through close observation, the speaker has realized this creature's amazing ability to survive despite repeated attempts to capture it (she describes the "five big hooks / grown firmly in his mouth"). Detail by detail, Bishop builds a case for the fish as majestic, and in admiration, she lets it go.

In every successful poem, there is some kind of tension, some torque. In "Grief," there is the grief that "shrieks," that petitions God, set against silent, "moveless woe." "The Body Mutinies" hovers between health and illness, life and death. "Blandeur" sets itself against the immensities of life. And "The Fish" demonstrates the struggle for survival.

Robert Wrigley talks about tension this way:

> What triggers the poem—the object; the incident, real or imagined; the rhythmical phrases—will only take you (or perhaps I should say "me") so far, unless you uncover the possibility of further complexity. Unless you locate some kind of essential and unforeseen tension.

Essential and unforeseen. The poem needs to move the writer as well as the reader. James Tate said, "What we want from poetry is to be moved, to be moved from where we now stand. We don't just want to have our ideas and emotions confirmed."

So we need to challenge our own assumptions, to push into new and surprising territory. That may mean considering not only the poem's idea, but its opposite—or its several alternatives. It may mean asking questions you'll have no answers for. Always, it will mean acknowledging life's complexities, and our own mixed natures. If we are truthful with ourselves, we recognize that love may be shot through with resentment, admiration with envy or belittlement. The victim or martyr may take perverse pride in assuming that role. The qualities we despise in others are often those we struggle with in ourselves. In times of profound grief, joy may suddenly, irrepressibly and against all reason, fill us with the presence of life. Good poems are not simply recordings of these truths: they are flowerings in the consciousness of both writer and reader.

some exercises

1. Think about some truths you currently hold: People are inherently good. You can always rely on your friends. Love never lasts. Can you write a more specific, surprising statement about one of your truths? Robert Hass, in "Thin Air," writes of "how love fails in our well-meaning hands." Instead of saying, "We're all alike on the inside," Walt Whitman writes, "Thou reader throbbest life and pride and love the same as I." Jot down some possible ways to state one of your truths. Your first passes will likely be predictable. So dig deeper. Once you have a statement that feels fresh, use it as your opening and then "prove" your truth with specific examples.

   Now write another poem, opening with the same line. This time, try to *disprove* that statement by presenting the arguments against it.

   Finally, write a third poem that argues for *and* against your statement.
2. Write a prayer, even if you aren't religious. Begin with the word "Let . . ." to introduce a general wish, like Ryan's "Let less happen": Let our love have no end. Let peace be possible. Let joy draw

near. Rework your statement if necessary. Once you feel you have a strong opening, write a series of more specific restatements of your prayer, which intensify as you go.

3. *Epiphany* comes from the Greek for "appearance" or "revelation." The dictionary defines epiphany as "a sudden, intuitive perception of or insight into the reality or essential meaning of something, usually initiated by some simple, homely, or commonplace occurrence or experience." Write a poem describing such an experience, and close with an insight. Read "A Blessing" by James Wright and "Archaic Torso of Apollo" by Rainer Marie Rilke, two excellent examples of poems that end with an epiphany.
4. Narrative: Describe a series of events from your past. And then this happened, and then that, and then a third thing. What's the point of your narrative? Do a version in which, somewhere in the poem, you reveal the point of your story directly. Write another version in which you suggest the meaning of the story through imagery. In a third version, change the main point of the story. You'll likely find yourself changing details as you go, to accommodate this new direction.
5. Circular: Begin with an image or statement. Close with that same image or statement. Something has to have happened in between to make us understand the same words or image differently by the time we get to the end.
6. Open with a specific question: about your life, about the natural world, about political realities. Write two poems: one in which you come to a conclusion, and one in which you don't.

THE HOLY LONGING

Tell a wise person, or else keep silent,
because the massman will mock it right away.
I praise what is truly alive,
what longs to be burned to death.

In the calm water of the love-nights,
where you were begotten, where you have begotten,
a strange feeling comes over you
when you see the silent candle burning.

Now you are no longer caught
in the obsession with darkness,
and a desire for higher love-making
sweeps you upward.

Distance does not make you falter,
now, arriving in magic, flying,
and finally, insane for the light,
you are the butterfly and you are gone.

And so long as you haven't experienced
this: to die and so to grow,
you are only a troubled guest
on the dark earth.

—Johann Wolfgang von Goethe,
translated by Robert Bly

⁜ 26

metaphor 2: parts & the whole

Metaphor is more than simply one part of a whole poem. Sometimes it *is* the whole, the overriding image that holds the poem together. When a metaphor operates in this way, it's called a *conceit.* "King of the River," by Stanley Kunitz, illustrates how a writer threads a metaphor through an entire poem. This beautiful piece about aging and death comes from Kunitz's collection *Passing Through.* Here, the conceit is that a human is a dying salmon, "slipped out of your skin, / nosing upstream." Kunitz doesn't come out and say, "We are like the salmon"; he doesn't need to. He draws the comparisons movingly and achieves a great depth of feeling. (A *depth* of feeling; a *fathom* of feeling.) This is a poem well worth studying for its hypnotic cadences, gorgeous imagery, and intense spiritual questioning.

This Emily Dickinson poem offers another example of a conceit:

My Life had stood—a Loaded Gun—
In Corners—till a Day
The Owner passed—identified—
And carried Me away—

And now We roam in Sovereign Woods—
And now We hunt the Doe—
And every time I speak for Him—
The Mountains straight reply—

And do I smile, such cordial light
Upon the Valley glow—
It is as if a Vesuvian face
Had let its pleasure through—

And when at Night—Our good Day done—
I guard My Master's Head—
Tis better than the Eider-Duck's
Deep Pillow—to have shared—

To foe of His—I'm deadly foe—
None stir the second time—
On whom I lay a Yellow Eye—
Or an emphatic Thumb—

Though I than He—may longer live
He longer must—than I—
For I have but the power to kill,
Without—the power to die—

Although I can't easily paraphrase this poem, I feel its intensity. Who is the Owner in the poem? Maybe it's Dickinson's genius (or her juno).

There's a great sense of power once the speaker's life has been taken up by the Owner—an opportunity finally to discharge the pent-up energy of the loaded gun. It's a lethal energy. So is it creative energy? Creative and destructive at the same time? Is it an empowerment of self, or a giving up of self? Those are the questions I ask when I read it.

Further examples of metaphorical conceits can be found everywhere in your reading. After you've spent time with "King of the River," try these:

"The Silken Tent," Robert Frost
"Nick and the Candlestick," Sylvia Plath
"Her Kind," Anne Sexton
"Ithaca," C. P. Cavafy

See how the connection between the original subject and the conceit create the experience of the poem. Developing poems through metaphor enables these writers to embody their subjects in a richly textured world.

dazzle

Emily Dickinson also wrote:

Tell all the Truth but tell it slant—
Success in Circuit lies
Too bright for our infirm Delight
The Truth's superb surprise
As Lightning to the Children eased
With explanation kind
The Truth must dazzle gradually
Or every man be blind—

"The Truth must dazzle gradually." Zeus, the king of the Greek gods, manifested himself as lightning, hiding his full glory to avoid instantly vaporizing mere mortals. When you're dealing with intense emotions, metaphor is a powerful tool for "telling it slant." It can offer that "necessary coldness" so you can approach the material, and shape it. Reread Nick Flynn's "Bag of Mice," on pages 188–89. The conceit of the bag of mice scurrying over the "shorn field" is the gradual dazzlement Dickinson refers to. The description of the "carbon letters" of the mother's suicide note, burning, allow us to contemplate the ending of her life indirectly. The poem depends on creating a metaphorical world, rather than a literal one. Bottled lightning.

Take a powerful personal experience of losing someone through death, a breakup, or a separation. You must be ready to use this as poetic material.

Close your eyes. Think of all the objects you associate with that person: toothbrush, car, key chain, shirt, chair, necklace, box of tools, coin collection.

Make a quick list of those objects.

Now focus on one object.

In "Bag of Mice," Flynn focuses on the suicide note that is disappearing, burning.

Close your eyes again and imagine that your object is disappearing, and someone or something is making it disappear. How is it disappearing? Is it burning? Is it fading? Is it being broken into pieces? Is it being carried away? Who or what is making this object disappear? Is it Death? Is it God? Is it a careless child? Infuse the loss of the object with your feelings about the loss of this person.

If you like, imagine this object restored to you in some way. Write about its return.

sea of love

Ezra Pound cautioned writers against joining a concrete noun with an abstraction to create a metaphor like "sea of love" or "bed of desire." But poets have always conceived interesting metaphors this way, as in these lines from "Berkeley," by Tony Hoagland:

> Close your eyes,
> swing a baguette horizontally
> you'll hit someone with a Ph.D. in sensitivity,
> someone who,
> if not a therapist himself,
> will offer you the number of his therapist,
> which it may take you years
> to figure out is a hostile act on his part
> designed to send you on a wild-goose chase
> through the orchard of your childhood
> to fetch the tarnished apple of your mother's love.

"The orchard of your childhood," "the tarnished apple of your mother's love." One long sentence moves from the imperatives "Close your eyes, / swing a baguette" to a series of details, each one building on the previous language:

"Someone" is modified by "who, if not a therapist himself, will offer you the number of his therapist."

The act of offering is modified/extended by "which it may take you years to figure out is a hostile act on his part."

Next, that hostile act is further described; it's "designed to send you on a wild-goose chase."

But Hoagland doesn't stop there. He gives us the phrase "through the orchard of your childhood" and keeps going, "to fetch the tarnished apple of your mother's love."

This is admirable syntax as well as metaphor, building the sentence and furthering both the idea and its humor.

Play with this pairing of the abstract and concrete. Start by randomly mixing and matching from the lists below, or create your own list of concrete and abstract nouns.

airplane	grief
box	panic
piano	happiness
cup	desire
vulture	history
lost dog	humiliation
skillet	death
shot glass	perfect love
snake	unrequited love
shark	anxiety
egg	hopelessness
umbrella	envy
river	silence
rat	ignorance
city	poverty
mountain	kindness

In developing the metaphor, use specifics. How would the lost dog of perfect love behave? What might be inside the egg of history? The words can be more specific, too: not "an airplane of death" but "the C-130 delivering its cargo of sudden death"; not "the river of grief" but "the filthy Ganges that carries my grief." If you want to play with an idea like "river of grief" without using the construction Pound deplored, you might say,

"The sluggish river moves through me, carrying your memory." You've suggested grief or a person's death, without spelling it out.

metonymy and synecdoche

I can never keep these two terms straight, but they are useful, and fascinating, strategies. The first is *metonymy:* substituting one thing for another with which it's commonly associated. When we say, "The pen is mightier than the sword," we're saying that writing and reason are stronger than killing and war. Writers use pens; soldiers use swords. (Now I suppose you'd have to say the laptop is mightier than the bunker buster, and how great it would be if that were true.) Hitler's storm troopers were known as the brownshirts because of their uniforms. Men and women in the corporate world are sometimes referred to as suits.

Other examples of metonymy:

Will there be any *big names* at the event? (Names are associated with people.)

He's a man *of the cloth.* (For the priest's vestments.)

He was a *hired gun.* (For the weapon used.)

Here's an interesting case:

I drank the whole *bottle.* (The bottle is still there; what's meant is I drank all the wine, or whiskey, or whatever was inside the bottle. We use "book" in a similar way when we mean what is inside. For example: "That book was good," or "I didn't understand that book," are examples of metonymy. But "That book could be used as a doorstop, it's so big and heavy" is literal.)

When you call someone a hayseed, you're using metonymy to show he's unsophisticated—a rural rather than an urban person.

On the other hand, if you call him an asshole, this is *synecdoche:* substituting the part for the whole.

You can also substitute the whole for the part, as in, "He thinks the world has treated him badly."

More examples of synecdoche:

I got a new *set of wheels* (I got a new car).

They drove in *twenty heads* of cattle. (There were twenty cattle, not just twenty heads.)

Notice how Ellen Bryant Voigt's poem "*Variations*: Two Trees" employs synecdoche:

> Because it is a curse to be beautiful
> and thus dismissed by other men,
> the pretty man often wants to marry
> mind, or grit, or great heart undistracted.

I wonder if she's right about that. The pretty men I've known have always gone for pretty women—or other pretty men. In any case, the last line is where the metaphor kicks in. Someone's mind is a part of her—the assertion is not that a pretty man wants to marry a mind, but to marry someone who has a mind (presumably a good one). "Great heart" is another example of synecdoche, since the heart is part of a person. (And when we say someone has "heart" in this way, of course we mean it metaphorically.)

Here's an exercise in metonymy. Start by describing an observed or remembered scene that involves conflict or tension: people arguing in a parking lot, a mother scolding her child, a partner who won't do the dishes or run an errand. Write about that scene and then see if you can liven things up with metonymy. This will mean thinking hard about associations.

Here is my rendering of the exercise:

> Friday after Turkey Day:
> the platters have all been carved and served.
> The wallets and purses
> are waiting in line at Macy's at 7 A.M.

for the doors to swing open, like the gates
to a bargain heaven. Choirs of halos
are singing. When the doors
close at ten, the last shopping bags
will hurry down the street, past
the carts sleeping in doorways,
the worn shoes and smelly coats, the bottles
asleep on their sides, tucked into paper bags.

Metonymy: Turkey Day for Thanksgiving; platters for turkeys; wallets and purses for shoppers; halos for angels, or possibly children singing carols; shopping bags for people; carts, etc., for homeless people (some of these images might also qualify as *personification*—giving human qualities to objects).

Now describe the same scene using synecdoche. This might be more challenging—it was for me, at least. Here's my rewrite:

When the doors close at Macy's,
all that humanity
will hurry down the street, past
the chapped and reddened faces sleeping in doorways,
past the yellowed toenails, the labels of Thunderbird
and Night Train curled asleep on their sides.

"Humanity" substitutes the whole for the part (individual people). Then there are the "faces" and "yellowed toenails" sleeping, parts for the whole. The brand labels, too, are parts of the bottles.

When you try these exercises, things may get confusing; metaphor enmeshes you in the complexities of language. But it can also open up your writing and thinking in unexpected directions. To fall down the rabbit hole of metaphor is always an adventure.

✳ 27

enchantments: myths & fairy tales

When I was little, and my mother read me fairy tales, she told me I would outgrow them one day. I did go on to other reading, other stories. But I never lost my taste for magic and unlikely occurrences, for worlds fraught with evil and danger and people trying to do good, worlds in which anything might happen. Worlds, that is, much like the one we live in.

In *The Uses of Enchantment*, psychologist Bruno Bettelheim said that fairy tales, for children, are psychic journeys—opportunities to confront the fears and intuitions of childhood in a form that's manageable. Terrible things happen in fairy tales. Even in the watered-down Disney versions, stepmothers try to poison their stepdaughters, children are lost in the woods and captured to be eaten, young women are imprisoned in towers. These stories have fascinated adults as well as children because of their symbolism, their portrayal of men and women, morality and ethics. They're rich with human drama.

The same is true of myths. The Greek and Roman gods, for all their divinity, acted a lot like human beings. They loved the wrong people, became enraged and jealous, punished those who displeased them. Whether you read the Bible, Native American creation stories, Celtic myths, or the Bhagavad-Gita, what emerges is the imprint of the human situation.

It's human nature not only to invent stories to explain the world, but also to retell the old stories. We're recyclers. Early Christians recast pagan traditions and rituals, giving them new meanings. Shakespeare's plays were based on earlier stories. The *Star Wars* movies were shaped by George Lucas's reading of Joseph Campbell's *The Hero with a Thousand Faces*—a book that tracked the similarity of the hero's journey across myths and religions throughout history. The hero is Ulysses or Moses or Gilgamesh or Wolverine. The journey of Orpheus to the underworld follows the same pattern as the Native American shaman's.

Any story you have to tell has been told before. "I fell in love the minute I saw him." "She hurt me so badly I wanted to die." "My mother's jealous of me." "I felt as if this was the thing that would make me a man." These are old stories. They become interesting when you make them yours, using the details of your life or your imagination, or both.

There's a reason so many poems refer to Persephone or Zeus or Sleeping Beauty. The truth of the old story continues in new guises that transform it. If your readers are familiar with some of the details of the story, they can take pleasure in seeing how you've accomplished this transformation.

Louise Glück's "Gretel in Darkness," countering the rosy ending of the fairy tale, gives us a Gretel still traumatized years after her ordeal in the forest. The harmful women, the stepmother and witch, are dead. But Gretel seems to long for a mother. Glück sets her clearly apart from the men in the story, the protective father and the brother she "killed for."

Using the known story, Glück powerfully portrays a psyche haunted by terrifying memories.

> This is the world we wanted.
> All who would have seen us dead
> are dead. I hear the witch's cry
> break in the moonlight through a sheet
> of sugar: God rewards.
> Her tongue shrivels into gas . . .
>
> Now, far from women's arms
> and memory of women, in our father's hut
> we sleep, are never hungry.
> Why do I not forget?
> My father bars the door, bars harm
> from this house, and it is years.
>
> No one remembers. Even you, my brother,
> summer afternoons you look at me as though
> you meant to leave,
> as though it never happened.
> But I killed for you.
> I see armed firs,
> the spires of that gleaming kiln—
>
> Nights I turn to you to hold me
> but you are not there.
> Am I alone? Spies
> hiss in the stillness, Hansel,
> we are there still, and it is real, real,
> that black forest, and the fire in earnest.

Robert Coover's short novel *Briar Rose* is about storytelling as much as the romantic fantasies and projections of the sleeping princess and the prince trying to hack his way through the briars. Coover's *Stepmother* is a brilliant, manic invasion of all kinds of tales, and takes place in a woods full of sorcerers, witches, charms, potions, and supernatural creatures under every magic stone.

In Anne Sexton's *Transformations,* you can see how her concerns—the female body, love, motherhood, morality—found expression. Sexton filtered Grimm's fairy tales through a twentieth-century female sensibility, updating them, redrawing characters and endings. Derek Walcott's *Omeros* transplants the Odyssey to St. Lucia, Walcott's native island in the Caribbean. In "Lady Lazarus," Sylvia Plath becomes a female Lazarus, raised from the dead to talk to the "peanut-crunching crowd" about suicide attempts. Anna Akhmatova reimagines Lot's wife looking back at the city she is leaving.

Doug Anderson, a Vietnam veteran, imagines his way into the Trojan War, creating a powerful, disturbing poem:

A BAR IN ARGOS

"They'll tell you it was a wooden horse;
I'll tell you it was not.
We gutted twenty oxen,
and slid inside their empty bellies,
but for our short-swords, naked;
then were sewn up, delivered to the city gates
as an offering of peace,
acquiescent to Troy's enduring power
and that night while the cooks made the fires
to roast the beasts with us as stuffing,
we cut the rawhide sutures

and were born out of the stink and slime,
killing first the cooks, headfirst in their vats,
their legs kicking, then moving
through the streets garroting sentries,
dowsing their torches in puddles,
killing blindly—twice killing our own—
catching Trojans in their beds,
and Odysseus, ecstatic, almost forgetting
to open the city gates; the high point of his night
when with a pike he pinned a woman to her bed
right through her lover's back.
I tell you I was sick, still am, it rots your soul;
it's just that anything you think is twisted
Odysseus can give another twist
you wouldn't think was there to give.
I tell you the man's a son of a bitch.
Wooden horse? Fuck me!
We were shat out of oxen to win that war."

This story could be the story of any soldier, in any war—recalling atrocities, complaining about his commanding officer and the "official" story that sanitizes what really happened. If you are marginally acquainted with the *Odyssey*, you can appreciate how Anderson rewrites not only the story of the Greeks and the Trojan horse, but also the character of Odysseus. The focus of the story is not the hero, but the grunt under his command.

From the margins, the world looks different.

the stories you know

If you're familiar with Greek and Roman mythology, that can be a source of subject matter for you. Fairy tales, comic books, cartoons, and movies have all portrayed memorable heroes and villains. A poem based on any of these might be tragic or funny or ironic; the key is to imbue a known story with your sensibility. Here are some strategies to do just that.

A Moment of Decision

Write about the main character of the story at the moment of making a decision. Use close third person to explore this point of view—"he" or "she," "Eve" or "Beavis"—to reveal the character's thoughts. Go ahead and give Beavis, of the nineties MTV show *Beavis and Butt-Head,* an inner life.

From the Margins

Write about a minor character in the story who doesn't usually receive much attention: one of the stepsisters in Cinderella, or the rat footman. Rewrite "Jack and the Beanstalk" from the point of view of the giant, or Jack's mother. Use first person.

Alternate Universe

Sexton's *Transformations* adapted fairy tales from the Brothers Grimm and made them contemporary. Cinderella, Rumpelstiltskin, Little Red Riding Hood, and other familiar characters coexist with Muzak, Christian Dior, diapers, and "middle-aged spread." Take an old story and update the characters, their surroundings, their language and attitudes. How about Helen of Troy as an exotic dancer? What if Hansel and Gretel got lost at the Mall of America in Minnesota? Put Barbie in a twelve-step program, or imagine she's in love with another Barbie. Put the biblical Lilith back in Adam's life. Put Martha Stewart in a cottage with the Seven Dwarfs, and have her show them how to freeze edible flowers in ice cube trays.

Character Is Destiny
This is where you can make Odysseus a coward, or portray Snow White as an obsessive-compulsive. In "Flames," by Billy Collins, Smoky the Bear, sick of "the half-wit camper" and "the dumbbell hiker," is recast as an arsonist. Maybe Aunt Jemima, the prototype of the black "mammy," is sick of pancakes and tired of smiling at white people. Suppose Peter Pan leaves the Lost Boys, enlists in the Marines, and goes to war in the Middle East.

The stories you know have infinite possibilities for becoming other stories.

the stories you may not know

Pick a myth you have heard of but don't know well; the details of the story are vague to you. A Greek or Roman myth, a traditional Japanese or Celtic folktale, the X-Men or Lara Croft, Tomb Raider. Learn that story, and then write your own poem, using any of the suggestions above.

Every group of people has its myths and folktales. Learn a story you connect to in some way, and then recast it. If you're African-American, you might look at Zora Neale Hurston's *Every Tongue Got to Confess: Negro Folk-Tales from the Gulf States,* vivid stories from the early black experience in America. Maybe you have a housemate from Iran and you're curious about Persian myths. Or you live in the Southwest and are fascinated by Hopi or Navajo stories. (Denise Duhamel, in a book called *The Woman with Two Vaginas*, retells Inuit stories—many of them hilarious, all of them about sex. I was amazed that the Inuits thought so much about sex. "Oh, they had other stories," Denise told me. "I just picked the sexual ones.")

the stories you invent

Writers are gods; they can create whole worlds. When you write a story, you set the terms. You can put a self-serving politician in a lower circle of hell, or in a prison cell. You can create a world without war, or one in which all children have wings and fly until the age of twelve or thirteen, when the wings shrivel and drop off. A world in which animals talk, and keep humans for pets.

Anything is possible in your head.

The trick is making a reader "believe" it. The more fantastic the story, the more we need physical detail to ground us. If you read science fiction, you know how intricate the worlds of sci-fi are. And when your premise is unlikely or surreal, you need to convince us with the texture of reality—as Russell Edson does in this prose poem:

BABY PIANOS

A piano had made a huge manure. Its handler hoped the lady of the house wouldn't notice.

But the lady of the house said, what is that huge darkness?

The piano just had a baby, said the handler.

But I don't see any keys, said the lady of the house.

They come in later, like baby teeth, said the handler.

Meanwhile the piano had dropped another huge manure.

What's that, cried the lady of the house, surely not another baby?

Twins, said the handler.

They look more like cannon balls than baby pianos, said the lady of the house.

The piano dropped another huge manure.

Triplets, smiled the handler . . .

What a great poem about art. The piano—this lovely musical instrument, hallmark of a civilized home, is, in Edson's piece, a dangerous animal that craps on the floor and requires a handler. The handler "explains" the piano's behavior in comforting terms: the "huge darkness" that the woman (tellingly, the "lady of the house") sees is only a baby. As the evidence piles up, so to speak, the lady of the house begins to realize the danger. "They look more like cannonballs . . ." The handler sounds even more menacing as he blithely assures her that all is well. Russell portrays the kind of people who invite art into their homes and expect it to be pretty and decorous, never disturbing. I'm reminded of the controversy over funding for the National Endowment for the Arts in the early 1990s. Many people thought government support of the arts was a good idea, until they saw some of the projects that were funded (such as Andres Serrano's *Piss Christ,* a photograph of a crucifix submerged in the artist's urine).

Write a prose poem with a fantastic premise. Any of these lines may get you started. Or come up with your own.

- My father is growing wings.
- On the day my mother died, the faucet in the kitchen began dripping milk.
- In the middle of the argument with my wife, the cat padded in and told us to shut the fuck up.
- The horse on the balcony is getting to be a problem.
- One bright day in the middle of the night, two dead boys got up to fight. (This is one of my favorites from childhood. The next line is "Back to back they faced each other, drew their swords and shot each other.")
- My smile won't come off, no matter how hard I scrub.
- One day all the trees in my neighborhood pulled themselves up by the roots and walked away.

IV.
toward mastery

✳ 28

music & meter

Until the twentieth century, when a group of poets championed free verse and caused a shift in American poetic practice, meter—from the Greek for "measure"—was the basis for most poetry written in English. When we speak of the meter of a poem, we're referring to the arrangement of sounds in set patterns: stressed and unstressed syllables in lines of a certain length. (Say the word "meter" and you'll hear it as a stressed syllable followed by an unstressed one: ME-ter.) If you came to poetry the way I did—discovering free-verse poems and trying to write my own versions—you may be in the dark about meter, as I was. Or you may have learned, and forgotten, exactly what "iambic pentameter" means, though you know it's important—iambic pentameter has been the predominant meter since the fourteenth century. Without an understanding of meter, you can't fully appreciate the tradition of literature in English.

Meter is challenging for many people. They can't hear where the stressed syllable falls in a word like "burning." (You should hear it as BURN-ing. The dictionary can also tell you which syllables in a word are stressed.) Or they find it difficult to find the stresses in a line of poetry. (Say aloud, "The forest was burning rapidly." You may be tempted not to stress "burning," because the word "rapidly" seems to have a stronger stress: "The FOR-est was burn-ing RAP-id-ly." However, "burning" should receive a stress in the first syllable as usual.)

Tune in to the sounds of language. This applies to not only to metrical lines, but also to vowels and consonants, to the effects of line breaks and punctuation. Reading poems aloud is one way to develop your ear. For the deaf or hearing-impaired, something different may be operating; the "unheard melodies" that Keats referred to in "Ode on a Grecian Urn" are clearly there, for there have been several deaf poets—including some who don't write, but instead compose their poems in sign language. When I read silently, I hear words in my head. Sometimes it's surprising to hear poems in the voices of their writers, because the voices in my head are so different. The first time I heard a recording of Sylvia Plath, I was stunned; she wasn't *my* Plath. It took a while to get used to how her poems sounded in her voice.

Study the rhythms of lines, metrical or not. Pay attention to how quickly or slowly the line goes, whether it feels like a bunch of marbles in your mouth or a long pour of clover honey. Notice echoes. Rhyme is an obvious echo, one word calling to another. In subtler ways, words can also whisper to each other.

Here are lines from *Leaves of Grass* by Walt Whitman, some of them explicitly about sounds. They aren't in meter—breaking from nineteenth-century metrical conventions was one of his many innovations—but they are acutely sensitive to the music of language.

The little one sleeps in its cradle;
I lift the gauze and look a long time, and silently brush away flies
with my hand.

The youngster and the red-faced girl turn aside up the bushy hill,
I peeringly view them from the top.

The suicide sprawls on the bloody floor of the bedroom,
I witness the corpse with its dabbled hair, I note where the pistol has
fallen.

The blab of the pave, the tires of carts, sluff of boot-soles, talk of the
promenaders,
The heavy omnibus, the driver with his interrogating thumb, the
clank of the shod horses on the granite floor,
The snow-sleighs, clinking, shouted jokes, pelts of snow-balls,
The hurrahs for popular favorites, the fury of rous'd mobs,
The flap of the curtain'd litter, a sick man inside borne to the
hospital,
The meeting of enemies, the sudden oath, the blows and fall,
The excited crowd, the policeman with his star quickly working his
passage to the centre of the crowd,
The impassive stones that receive and return so many echoes,
What groans of over-fed or half-starv'd who fall sunstruck or in fits,
What exclamations of women taken suddenly who hurry home and
give birth to babes,
What living and buried speech is always vibrating here, what howls
restrain'd by decorum,
Arrests of criminals, slights, adulterous offers made, acceptances,
rejections with convex lips,
I mind them or the show or resonance of them—I come and I depart.

How quickly these scenes of nineteenth-century America come alive, carried from Whitman's ears and eyes to ours. Listen, for example, in that fifth line, to the *s* sounds in "suicide" and "sprawls"; to the *d*'s in "suicide," "bloody," and "bedroom"; the *b*'s in "bloody" and "bedroom." Then there's "sprawls" and "bloody" and "floor."

And we haven't even gotten to the stresses in the line: the SU-icide SPRAWLS on the BLOOD-y FLOOR of the BED-room.

Or to how the line begins with vowels in the high register and (mostly) moves lower. If you delete the consonants, the line sounds something like *ooh-eye-aw-uh-ee-uh-aw-ed-ooh.*

And that's just one line.

See the difference if Whitman had written,

> On the bloody floor of the bedroom, the suicide sprawls.

or

> On the bloody floor of the bedroom sprawls the suicide.

The syntax has changed; in some way the meaning has changed, too. (I like what someone once said about meaning: that it is everything you get from the poem.) Change the music, and you change the meaning.

Whitman had a great ear. He listened not only to the sounds of the street—the "blab" of the pave, the "sluff" of boot-soles, the "flap" of the curtain'd litter—but to the rhythmic patterns of the King James Bible, where *parallel structure* was an important principle. Parallel structures are similar patterns—of words, phrases, or clauses. Here are two examples of parallel clauses from the Bible:

> The wilderness and the solitary place shall be glad for them; and
> the desert shall rejoice, and blossom as the rose.
>
> —*Isaiah 35:1*

For my yoke is easy, and my burden is light.

—*Matthew 11:30*

Each of these sentences falls neatly into two parts, on either side of the semicolon and comma. In each case we have a subject or subjects, followed by future-tense verbs in the first sentence, and present-tense verbs in the second. That's grammatical parallelism. Parallel structure can refer to meaning as well; the wilderness that "shall be glad" is similar to the desert that "shall rejoice." "Yoke" is parallel to "burden," and "easy" has a similar meaning to "light." In another kind of parallel structure (there are several), each half of the sentence might represent an opposite. Parallel structure is all about balance.

You can see how Whitman adapted this strategy. "I witness the corpse with its dabbled hair, I note where the pistol has fallen." Whitman read the Bible and listened to the music of Hebrew verse in translation, and as any good musician would, he used what he heard to fashion his own style. Just as you can find in jazz the influence of the blues, and find in the origins of the blues English ballads and African call-and-response, you can trace writers' influences. Allen Ginsberg will lead you back to Walt Whitman, to William Blake and other poets. Contemporary poet Jack Gilbert will lead you back to classical Chinese poets like Wang Wei and Tu Fu, whom he read and admired for their clarity.

The more you discern the music of other poets, the more you can draw on what they've done.

Studying metrical verse is excellent ear training. It focuses you on rhythmic patterns (and their variations, as you'll soon see), and offers you a concrete way to explore those patterns. Meter is highly organized rhythm, a way to maintain the beat. Once you can find the beat, you can hear the departures from it as well.

I'll give you an example, the opening of a poem by John Donne, one of his "Holy Sonnets" (number 14):

Batter my heart, three-person'd God ; for You
As yet but knock, breathe, shine, and seek to mend ;
That I may rise and stand, o'erthrow me, and bend
Your force to break, blow, burn, and make me new.

The "beat" of this poem is iambic pentameter. An iamb is an unstressed syllable followed by a stressed one: da-DUM. In iambic pentameter, there are five iambs in each line. Even if you can't yet hear that underlying pattern, you're probably hearing many of the rhythms—how, for example, the three stresses of KNOCK, BREATHE, SHINE are echoed in BREAK, BLOW, BURN. You might notice, too, that the meanings and sounds of the first three words are a little "softer" than the meanings and sounds of the second three. Or maybe it's more accurate to say that the second three words are harder—"break" is harder than "knock," "blow" more forceful and quicker in the mouth than "breathe," to "burn" is more powerful than to "shine." You'd probably also pick up on the end rhymes of *you-mend-bend-new*. And further, you might see that the lines are pretty much the same length. In fact, three of the lines have ten syllables, and one eleven syllables.

This is already a lot to take in.

The traditional sonnet has a rhyme scheme (a pattern of rhymes at the ends of the lines) and is written in iambic pentameter. It's crucial that you recognize this beat. Without it, you miss a high level of beauty in a lot of poetry.

The beat, or the meter, is what I call the ghost in the machine. It's there, but it's not there. If you read the first line of the Donne aloud, it doesn't quite sound like da-DUM da-DUM da-DUM da-DUM da-DUM.

This is where things get interesting.

The trick in meter is to hear, under:

BAT-ter my HEART, THREE-PERson'd GOD, for YOU,

bat-TER my HEART, three-PERson'd GOD, for YOU

Say the two lines aloud. The first indicates how we would actually say the words. "Batter" is pronounced with the accent on the first syllable. BAT-ter.

In the second line, I've shown you the beat.

When you set words *as they are actually said* against *the expectation of the beat,* you are experiencing the beauty of meter. In the first line, because we know this is a sonnet, because we expect the iambic pentameter line to begin da-DUM, we get a little jolt: DA-dum. *Batter* my heart. Don't just knock. I need you to break down my door. The poem is a prayer to God for transformation: Make me new. To substitute DA-dum (a pattern called a *trochee*) where an iamb should be makes us sit up and pay attention. In line three, we get something else instead of an iamb when Donne writes,

> As YET but KNOCK, BREATHE, SHINE, and SEEK to MEND

So "knock, breathe, shine" stands out. As it needs to, so this effect can recur in the fourth line with "break, blow, burn."

And then there's line three, the one with the extra syllable, which so brilliantly marries music to meaning. The first part of the line fits the beat perfectly, making the word "o'erthrow" (overthrow) so much more powerful:

> That I may RISE and STAND, O'ERTHROW me, and BEND

Not only does Donne put in an extra syllable at that point, he also makes it a stressed one. Where we expect a simple da-DUM, we get instead: *O'erthrow* me. Don't be nice. I need to be overthrown, overpowered, ravished. (The poem ends, "Nor ever chaste, except you ravish me.")

The sonnet is a powerful form. It can sing of desire and anger and envy and grief. In the hands of a writer with a good ear, it can batter your heart.

What makes a good musician, in addition to a good ear? In a word: practice. Hours and hours of it. Scales, finger exercises, breathing exercises, whatever the instrument requires. I used to practice my flute a minimum of three hours a day. Now that I play blues harmonica, I practice as often as I can. Professional musicians have usually spent several years putting in eight-hour days on their instruments. In music, you can see that the time you put in translates into greater ability. Your tone gets better, you can play a scale faster, you memorize licks and improvise ideas around chord changes until it all starts to flow. You start out clumsy—you expect to—and you practice.

For writing, it's the same. If you don't practice—a lot—you won't improve. Or you may improve so slowly that you give up in frustration.

Here are the common building blocks of meter, and some ways to practice with them:

(double meters)
Iamb: da-DUM. Implode, or else, deny, forget, hello
trochee: DA-dum. Happy, crazy, apple, sordid, mantra, cocktail
spondee: DA-DA. Real world, hard times, bank heist, got milk?

(triple meters)
anapest: da-da-DUM. Bada-bing, at the top, underneath, in a pinch
dactyl: DA-da-da. Excellent, honesty, calendar, neighborhood, daffodil
amphibrach: da-DA-da. Inhaler, excitement, your mama, believer

monometer—one foot per line
dimeter—two feet per line
trimeter—three feet per line

tetrameter—four feet per line
pentameter—five feet per line
hexameter—six feet per line
heptameter—seven feet per line

Ear Training Practice

Notice the language in your immediate world. Listen for words or phrases that are iambs, trochees, dactyls, etc.: the spondee of "Car Wash"; the church marquee that reads SERVICE TONIGHT, a trochee followed by an iamb. If there is a friend or fellow writer handy, you can play word association, with a twist: Each word has to be a metrical foot. If you were to choose dactyls, a back-and-forth might run: *fingernail-manicure-pedicure-hairdresser-Goldilocks.*

You can practice with a group as well. Or try this: Choose a metrical foot, go around the room and see how quickly each person can come up with a word that fits. The faster the better. (Those are trochees.) *Better, faster, harder, larder, future, anger.* (A good mnemonic for the trochee is that it *is* one.)

Once you're finished with metrical feet, see if the group, or you and another person, can generate a line of iambic pentameter: five iambs that make sense as a line. This is more challenging, and also more fun.

Try generating several lines to write a group poem this way.

Writing Practice

- Write five lines of trochaic dimeter (two trochees in each line).
  Here's a jump-rope rhyme I remember from childhood, which contains some variations after the fourth line:

  Cinderella
  Dressed in yellow
  Went upstairs to

Kiss a fellow
Made a mistake
Kissed a snake
How many doctors
Did it take?

- Write five lines of iambic trimeter (three iambs in each line). Read "My Papa's Waltz" by Theodore Roethke. Notice his departures from the strict da-DUM da-DUM da-DUM. Try to create your own meaningful departures.
- Write five lines of trochaic tetrameter. The refrain of the witches' chant in Shakespeare's *Macbeth* is one example:

Double, double, toil and trouble;
Fire burn, and cauldron bubble.

You can also reread Blake's "The Tyger" on pages 138–39.

- Write some ballad stanzas. These are four-line iambic stanzas that follow the pattern of four-three-four-three. Here is an anonymous English ballad, probably from the sixteenth century:

THE LOVER IN WINTER PLAINETH FOR THE SPRING

O western wind, when wilt thou blow
  That the small rain down can rain?
Christ, that my love were in my arms
  And I in my bed again!

Emily Dickinson is also an excellent model here. Many of her rhythms are based on Protestant hymns. If you know "The Yellow Rose of Texas," or the hymn "Amazing Grace," you'll easily connect with the pattern she uses. Here's a beautiful short Dickinson poem:

My life closed twice before its close—
It yet remains to see
If Immortality unveil
A third event to me

So huge, so hopeless to conceive
As these that twice befell.
Parting is all we know of heaven,
And all we need of hell.

- Blank verse is unrhymed iambic pentameter. This is the meter of Shakespeare's plays. Look at these famous lines from *Romeo and Juliet,* spoken by Romeo as he stands in the Capulets' orchard and sees a lit candle in Juliet's bedroom window:

But soft! What light from yonder window breaks?
It is the East, and Juliet is the sun!
Arise, fair sun, and kill the envious moon
Who is already sick and pale with grief
That thou her maid art far more fair than she.
Be not her maid, since she is envious.
Her vestal livery is but sick and green,
And none but fools do wear it. Cast it off.
It is my lady! O, it is my love!
O, that she knew she were!

Try some short poems in blank verse. These poems provide examples:

"Indian Boarding School: The Runaways," Louise Erdrich
"Sunday Morning" and "The Idea of Order at Key West,"
Wallace Stevens
"Birches" and "Directive," Robert Frost
"Ulysses," Alfred, Lord Tennyson

✳ 29

write a sonnet

The sonnet, which translates from the Italian as "little song," has a special status in poetry. Since its invention in Italy in the thirteenth century—its likely origins are an eight-line Sicilian song form called the *strambotto,* to which a poet added six lines—the sonnet has proven immensely popular. In the fourteenth century, the Italian poet Petrarch wrote love sonnets to Laura, a merchant's wife, detailing his passion and extolling her virtues. Dante followed with *La Vita Nuova,* which included sonnets to Beatrice—another unattainable woman who served as his muse not only for that book, but also for his *Divine Comedy.* From Italy, the sonnet swept over Europe, and arrived in England in the early sixteenth century. By the end of the century, when Shakespeare was writing, the Elizabethans were in the midst of a "sonnet craze."

It's due to previous writers' brilliant use of the form that we still read, and write, sonnets. Shakespeare and many other poets found the restrictions of fourteen lines, a meter and rhyme scheme, and the idea of a turn, or *volta*—which requires that whatever is set out in the first eight lines be amplified, or reconsidered, or countered, in the next six—to be heady challenges for the creative imagination.

Writing a sonnet will give you a better understanding of what all those great sonnet writers (not only Dante and Petrarch and Shakespeare, but also John Donne, George Herbert, Gerard Manley Hopkins, John Milton, John Keats, William Wordsworth, Elizabeth Barrett Browning, and Edna St. Vincent Millay, and many more) were up to. Writing a sonnet will teach you about economy, about structure, about how searching for a rhyme or following a rhythm can lead you into unexpected territory.

By this point, if you've been following the ideas and exercises in this book, you've had a chance to read several sonnets, and to learn one by heart. That's excellent preparation for writing one. Here are the technical details: The English, or Shakespearean, sonnet follows this rhyme scheme, or pattern of end rhymes: *abab, cdcd, efef, gg.* The Italian, also known as the Petrarchan, sonnet is more difficult: *abba, abba, cde, cde.* (The Italian language has more words that rhyme.) Elizabeth Barrett Browning's "Grief," on page 194, follows the Italian pattern. The meter of a sonnet is iambic pentameter; reread the sonnets in this book, and listen for that underlying beat.

A sonnet may follow an octave-sestet development, as "Grief" does. Or it may develop in three parallel quatrains, like Shakespeare's "Sonnet 73," on page 79. Shakespeare's speaker begins with a season, analogous to his physical state; then the ending of the day, describing his emotional state; and then his spiritual state: "In me thou see'st the glowing of such fire, / That on the ashes of his youth doth lie." The closing couplet of a Shakespearean sonnet, with its back-to-back rhymes, can also deliver an extra punch.

Though early sonnets were often vehicles for declarations of love—and have been used eloquently for that subject up to the present day—your sonnet needn't be about love. There are sonnets about war, illness, work, zoo animals, mammograms, bars, the personals. Anything can be subject matter.

Don't expect your first sonnets to be fabulous poetry. They may be silly, or corny, or clumsy, but you'll begin to appreciate the challenges and possibilities.

This contemporary sonnet by Marilyn Nelson shows just how fresh and immediate this eight-hundred-year-old form can be:

BALANCE

He watch her like a coonhound watch a tree.
What might explain the metamorphosis
he underwent when she paraded by
with tea-cakes, in her fresh and shabby dress?
(As one would carry water from a well—
straight-backed, high-headed, like a diadem,
with careful grace so that no drop will spill—
she balanced, almost brimming, her one name.)

She thinks she something, stuck-up island bitch.
Chopping wood, hanging laundry on the line,
and tantalizingly within his reach,
she honed his body's yearning to a keen,
sharp point. And on that point she balanced life.
That hoe Diverne think she Mares Tyler's wife.

Nelson's poem is part of a series, but creates an impact all its own, bringing to life a slave named Diverne, desired by her master (while the other slaves caustically comment in the italicized lines). The metered lines are lilting, never forced. Nelson shows that meter can be both speechlike and stately—and in the same poem. Her departures from the strict da-DUMs help us to see Diverne: "STRAIGHT-BACKED, HIGH-HEAD-ed, like a DI-a-dem." Notice how deftly Nelson uses rhyme, pairing "tree" with "by," "metamorphosis" with "dress," "diadem" with "name," "bitch" with "reach," "line" with "keen." In Shakespeare's time, strict rhyme was the norm. Today, a writer using rhyme is also likely to echo only the consonants in a word (called *consonance*), or the vowels (*assonance*). This creates richer, more varied possibilities; you don't have to rhyme "moon" with "June" (and since that's been done so often, you probably don't want to). Instead, try "fun," "sin," "moan," "gun," "station" (consonance), or "cool," "food," "you," "prove," "boot" (assonance).

Nelson withholds strict rhyme until her last two lines. The rhymes have kept us off-balance. In the end, Diverne balances between the two extremes, the white master's desire and the judgment of the other slaves.

Some contemporary writers have enjoyed playing fast and loose with the sonnet—showing us that they know the form, but taking off from it in satisfying ways. Denis Johnson talks about the end of love:

SWAY

Since I find you will no longer love,
from bar to bar in terror I shall move
past Forty-third and Halsted, Twenty-fourth
and Roosevelt where fire-gutted cars,
their bones the bones of coyote and hyena,
suffer the light from the wrestling arena
to fall all over them. And what they say
blends in the tarantellasmic sway
of all of us between the two of these:
harmony and divergence,
their sad story of harmony and divergence,
the story that begins

I did not know who she was
and ends *I did not know who she was.*

"Sway" gestures toward the sonnet's iambic pentameter, but doesn't always follow the meter. The harmonies of the sonnet are broken. The "turn" in the poem comes at the end of the ninth line, not the eighth. The rhyme scheme is *aa, bb, cc*—that is, couplet rhyme—until, significantly, the line that should rhyme with "two of these." At that point the rhymes diverge, just as the lovers have. The next line, "divergence," rhymes with the same word in the following line, bringing home the speaker's heart-broken awareness of the separate paths the lovers have taken. The last two lines repeat, carrying the obsessive tone even further. They bookend this relationship—any failed relationship.

Here are some exercises to help you develop your skill with the sonnet:

1. *Practice iambic pentameter* by recasting some lines from your journal—first in five strict da-DUMs, and then with slight variations. For example:
   "Another dreary Sunday morning. Looking out at the rain" might become, "On SUN-day MORN-ing RAIN is FAL-ling DOWN."
   Next you might arrive at "SUN-day MOR-ning, STAR-ing at the RAIN." That line begins with a dropped syllable, the unstressed syllable of the first iamb. And the fourth iamb, "-ing at," has turned into two unstressed syllables. That's the "ghost in the machine" I spoke of earlier, the underlying beat still there, but made less obvious by the variations.
2. *Write a deliberately bad sonnet.* Have fun with it; overwrite, use clichés, give each line five da-DUMs, and use strict rhyme. But see if you can develop a subject, and create a "turn" at the end of line eight. You can do this in a group as well, each person adding a line. You have fifteen minutes.

3. *Revise your sonnet.* Make it more subtle: a trochee substituted for an iamb, consonance or assonance instead of strict rhyme. If you have a lot of end-stopped lines, enjamb some of them.
4. *Innovate.* Once you can write a traditional sonnet, following the rules, you can break them. The key is this: The sonnet itself is now "the ghost in the machine." Although you're departing from it, the traditional sonnet still lurks in the background. A couplet sonnet, like Denis Johnson's "Sway," is one possibility. Here are others:

- A free-verse sonnet: no meter, but fourteen lines, a rhyme scheme, and a "turn" at the octet.
- A blank-verse sonnet. (Unrhymed iambic pentameter.)
- A reverse sonnet. Start with the couplet and go backwards. That means your sonnet will break into six and eight, rather than eight and six. Consider how this form might work with a particular subject.
- A sonnet-like poem. Keep only the concept of fourteen lines and the "turn."
- A form you invent, based on the sonnet. I invented the "sonnenizio": fourteen lines, no meter, no rhyme scheme. For a sonnenizio, start with a line from someone else's sonnet. Repeat one word from that line in every successive line of the poem. The last two lines have to rhyme.

One of my students, Clay Stockton, wrote this sonnenizio inspired by Shakespeare's Sonnet 173. The repeated word "leaves" goes through some clever permutations:

THE PICK-UP ARTIST IN SPRING

To love that well which thou must leave ere long
Sums up the romance thing if you believe,
As some do, that the yellow leaves do hang
To leave no doubt that loving means to grieve:

One always leaves. Some stay for just a week—
Spring break, perhaps—but sometimes leaving takes
A lifetime: two, in fact. The browned leaves seek
Relief on the ground, then in; the yellow shakes.

Against the cold? Not quite. Against the leaves'
Last lingering green, the spring that cleaves to them
Even as autumn's leave-taking bereaves
Their branches, leaving hope no cold can stem.

So, leaving first is the best choice you have.
And leave that well which soon enough you'd love.

✳ 30

a poem you love: close reading

In your reading and writing life, you'll likely discover many poems that you find powerful, moving, or transforming in some way. Read one of these poems over and over, just as you might if you were going to learn the poem by heart. As you read, notice what you're noticing. What strikes you about this poem—the music, the message, the feeling? Make notes for yourself, or read the poem to someone else and explain why you love it.

Close reading means that you pay attention to everything. As with a close friend or loved one, the more time you spend, the better you get to know that person. See if you realize something new after writing or talking about the poem.

Then you're really ready to take it apart.

It's impossible to kill a good poem. You won't ruin your experience of a good poem once you've dismantled it. Your appreciation can only increase. You will also find more ideas for your own work.

Here's a checklist for getting at what a poem is up to.

1. *The heart.* E. E. Cummings wrote, *since feeling is first*... This poem you love has a beating heart. What is it—the thing that drives the poem, that gives it some sense of urgency and causes you to laugh or nod in recognition or feel consolation in your grief? This attention is not only about identifying the emotion in the poem—which is probably clear to you—but about getting at the reason-for-being of this piece.
2. *The tone of voice.* Tone is tricky. The dominant mood or feeling may be fairly easy to identify, but there may be other things to notice. The voice of the writer may be different from the voice of the speaker in the poem (a good example is Robert Browning's "My Last Duchess," where we hear a self-satisfied creep talking about his mistress. Browning, the writer, obviously has a different attitude from the speaker). There may be more than one voice in a poem, as in John Berryman's "Dream Songs," which mix lofty diction with minstrel talk (from number 76: "In a modesty of death I join my father" and "You is from hunger, Mr. Bones") and oddly constructed sentences. Former Poet Laureate Robert Pinsky suggested that Berryman could get away with writing potentially sentimental or gassy statements by including other voices to deflate those statements. Diction, or word choice, is key to the poem's voice or voices. Is it *mama* or *mother*, *walk* or *dawdle* or *ambulate*? Philip Larkin's "Sad Steps" will also let you consider shifts in diction and the poet's reasons for doing so.
3. *The skeleton.* What's the structure of the piece? Where and how does the poem begin and end? Does it move outward from the first line, or circle back to an image or idea it opened with? Discover the turns—the places the poem moves away from the subject it has

introduced, or else delves more deeply into that subject. Does the poem open with an image, or a statement? How does it close? Pay attention to repeated images or ideas or phrases—where they surface, how they contribute to the whole.

4. *The body.* Here is where other matters of craft and technique come into play: line breaks, imagery, metaphor, rhythms. See how the line breaks function, notice the pacing of the poem as well as the unification or wild proliferation of metaphor and meaning. There may be mysterious lines, meanings you can't paraphrase, even after you try to decipher them.
5. *The syntax.* Syntax is so important to a poem's effects, yet we don't always focus on how sentences open, where they go, and how they get there. What is the relationship of long to short sentences, or sentences to fragments? There may be a characteristic syntax, in one poem or a number of poems by the writer. You may be surprised to find that syntax itself has drawn you to a poem. When I discovered the poetry of C. K. Williams, the syntax was one of the first things I noticed; I fell in love with his sentences.

31

page to stage: performance

> The mind is a wonderful thing—it starts working the minute you're born and never stops until you get up to speak in public.
>
> —*Roscoe Drummond*

Every poetry reading is theater. Every single one. Even if you are standing up there mumbling your poems, or forgetting a line of Shakespeare. Your reading may not be a great performance, but it's inescapably a performance.

Many poetry readings are excruciating precisely because the writer does not treat the reading as a bit of theater.

On the other hand, I've heard some great performers declaim some awful poetry.

When you read or recite poems, you are the focus of attention for a time span that is a part of the audience's life, and yours. You're there together, inhabiting the same space. Maybe it's only ten minutes. Maybe you'll never see each other again.

What do you want that experience to be?

Sometimes a poetry reading is a display of narcissism and ego: Look at me. I'm so outraged/sensitive/fucked up/heartbroken/brilliant. It can also be a place to claim your identity, to be part of a community. It can be an investigation of language and the heart's longings and our deep need to grapple with life's mysteries. It can be a celebration, entertainment, or a dutifully dull half hour everyone can't wait to escape from.

If the poetry is good, and the performer is doing his or her level best to get inside that poetry and share it with an audience, magic can happen.

Here's what I tell my students before their readings: The ear is very forgiving. The audience isn't there to take you apart. You've spent time working on your writing and your presentation. Neither may be as polished as you hoped, but that's okay. Amateur musicians get onstage at open mics in order to gain confidence and experience. They make some mistakes, and eventually get more professional. You can do the same.

Open mics are a great place for a poet to start. Virtually every city has at least one café or bookstore where people can read their work. If you live in a large city, there may be a dozen or more venues. By attending open mics, you can meet other people who are writing, gain encouragement, and develop both your writing and performance skills.

The first time I stood to recite my poems, I was terrified. No one booed me, and a couple of people even said, "Thanks for the poetry," as I left the stage, shaking. For quite a while, every time I read at an open mic, I had to have a couple of glasses of wine first. I was a terrible poet, and fortunately nobody told me how bad I was. I just forged ahead, a little high, reading my bad poems. Eventually I didn't need the wine, and my work got better. I still get very nervous sometimes before readings, but now I'm professional. I go on, I do my gig, I try to connect with the audience—that's the reason I'm there—and often it works. Sometimes the reading falls flat, and I know it. But I'm up there, so I keep going, and afterward I might have that wine.

Here are a few tips to keep in mind before you perform:

1. *Remember that it's natural to be nervous*, even to the point of sweating and dry mouth. Public speaking is one of the big fears. The adrenaline rush you experience is energy you can use. Practice and prepare, and then remind yourself that you have done so.
2. *Time yourself.* Don't wait until you're up there to wonder if you've got time to read two more. Time does funny things when you're performing. It can feel like half an hour when it's been five minutes, or vice versa. If you're giving a solo reading, be aware that after thirty-five to forty minutes, your audience is likely to grow restless. It's better to present a few well-chosen pieces than to wear out your welcome.
3. *Practice reading aloud.* Try different ways to deliver the poem, think about tone, pacing, volume. If you can get someone to listen to you and give you some pointers, even better. Or record yourself. It's common to read too quickly, so trying to slow down is a good idea.
4. *Have your poems ready.* Arrange the poems in the order you'll be reading them, in order to save shuffling papers or fumbling. If you want to leave room for inspiration, mark extra poems you might want to read.
5. *If you memorize your work, be sure you know the poems cold.* Practice in front of a mirror, so you can figure out how to stand without the props of paper or podium.
6. *Microphones can be intimidating.* If you don't know how to raise or lower the mike, ask for help. Then learn how to do it yourself, so the mike is level with your mouth and you don't have to stoop or stand on tiptoe. Don't get so close to the mike that you puncture eardrums, and don't stand so far back that no one can hear you. If

you're not sure whether you're at the right distance, ask the audience how you sound.

7. *Consider short introductions for some poems.* Remember, too, that silence is powerful. You might finish a poem and allow a pause before launching into the next. Try to avoid "My next poem is . . ."
8. *Focus on your work and your vision* (or the vision of the poet you are reciting) rather than yourself. Have faith in your work. You've honed it to the best of your ability. You're the instrument of the poetry; be as pure and effective an instrument as possible.
9. *Visualize the audience as your ally.* The audience is more like you than different from you. It may help, as Winston Churchill suggested, to visualize the audience naked. This will either make you feel more comfortable, or give you some erotic energy to run on. Having a friend or two in the crowd will also help; look to see where they're sitting. You can glance at them for encouragement.
10. *Relax.* Do some meditation or deep breathing before the performance.

✳ 32

word/art: make a broadside

Before newspapers, there were broadsides: sheets of paper printed with songs, religious tracts, gossip—whatever might sell—peddled in the streets. Sometimes the text was accompanied by illustrations, usually woodcuts. A contemporary broadside is likely to be a poem, sometimes letterpress-printed, often incorporating an image. A broadside of your own poem, or one of someone else's, can decorate your living space, or become a personalized gift. Combining words and images harks back to the origins of language, when alphabets were developed to create words that corresponded to visual symbols.

Here's a Chippewa song-picture from *Shaking the Pumpkin: Traditional Poetry of the Indian North Americas:*

SONG PICTURE #66 (a hunting song):

there's my war club
booming through the sky—
you animals better come when I call you

Kenneth Patchen, who pioneered reading poetry with jazz in the mid-twentieth century, created numerous picture poems—playful, vibrant paintings with poems written across them. They are online at a number of sites, including www.concentric.net/~lndb/patchen/patchclr.htm.

You may be inspired to make your own picture poem, even if, like me, you can only draw stick figures. If drawing just isn't your thing, cut out pictures and make a collage. Or use tracing paper, like the reclusive "outsider artist" Henry Darger, who traced figures from ads, then used them over and over with slight variations in his work. Darger also wrote thousands of pages. His work was discovered by his landlords after his death. You can see many Darger paintings online—they're vivid and disturbing. There's also *In the Realms of the Unreal,* a fascinating documentary about him.

Here are some possible ways to combine words and images:

- Select a work of art that interests you and add a short caption. Rather than writing the caption specifically for that art, look through free-writes in your journal for interesting phrases. Which of them might take the image in a new or surprising direction? Or choose several phrases. Type them out, cut a strip of paper for each phrase, and glue the phrases on a printout of the art. If you're a parent, you might caption your children's art.

- Another idea: Ask a visual artist to respond to lines of your poetry, or to an entire poem, with a drawing or painting or photograph. Print them together as a broadside.
- The photographer Duane Michaels often captioned his photographs, commenting on the subjects, talking about a particular moment. Go through your old photographs and caption them with a few lines that speak to the way you view them now.
- Make a collage using lines from favorite poems, mixed with photographs and/or magazine cutouts.
- Illustrate a short poem by someone else.
- Create a poem that unfolds in the form of a comic strip, alone or with a second poet/artist.
- Fool with the dimensionality of your work. Try out different textures of paper. What about other surfaces: a board where words and images can be drawn or painted, a box with words and glued-on figures and dried rose petals. What if you took a Barbie doll and wrote words all over it? You can put words on rocks or driftwood, or hang words like ornaments. At the Picasso Museum in Paris, I was struck by how Picasso used everything as a surface for art. Canvases, dishes, chairs—whatever was at hand. There are lots of ways to bring language off the page.

"WHAT DO WOMEN WANT?"

I want a red dress.
I want it flimsy and cheap,
I want it too tight, I want to wear it
until someone tears it off me.
I want it sleeveless and backless,
this dress, so no one has to guess
what's underneath. I want to walk down
the street past Thrifty's and the hardware store
with all those keys glittering in the window,
past Mr. and Mrs. Wong selling day-old
donuts in their cafe, past the Guerra brothers
slinging pigs from the truck and onto the dolly,
hoisting the slick snouts over their shoulders.
I want to walk like I'm the only
woman on earth and I can have my pick.
I want that red dress bad.
I want it to confirm
your worst fears about me,
to show you how little I care about you
or anything except what
I want. When I find it, I'll pull that garment
from its hanger like I'm choosing a body
to carry me into this world, through
the birth-cries and the love-cries too,
and I'll wear it like bones, like skin,
it'll be the goddamned
dress they'll bury me in.

--*Kim Addonizio*

--*illustration by Marcia Clay*

✳ 33

two heads: collaborations

Writing is a solitary occupation. While the rest of the world is out doing normal things, you are in a room somewhere exploring the contents of your head. You're casting about for an adjective, reworking a metaphor, or sitting and staring into space, wondering why you don't just get up and do something, *anything,* else. Making poems is hard work. You may feel burdened by the knowledge of all the great poems that have already been written, and the knowledge that it is going to take you years of study to come within shouting distance.

This is when having another person to share your pain, as well as the excitement of the process, can help. Your person could be another writer, someone to whom you show your work, who gives you feedback and shows his or her work in return. As great as it is to have a friend or family member listen to your poetry, that isn't the someone I'm talking about.

You need a colleague who thinks of writing as an art and a craft—or someone devoted to another art.

Who in your life could be this person? A fellow writing student, a painter, a photographer? Odds are there is someone in your life right now who could be your collaborator. Keep your eyes open for someone who might become your partner, and consider developing a project together.

In any creative person's life, there will be many projects. You may have already collaborated with an artist to make a broadside, or have asked a guitarist to play while you performed at an open mic. Those are excellent ways to begin to expand.

Here are some other possible ways to collaborate. But don't just try these suggestions; they're limited, because they're my ideas. Develop your own. Don't just think outside the box. Create a new box. Then break it open.

alternate lines

Here's an email project. One writer begins the poem, the second writer adds a line, and then it goes back to the first writer. You may want to agree on a limit, so you're both aware that the poem should go somewhere and end after a certain number of lines. Choose a subject that fires up both of you. Or, pick something one of you loves and the other hates.

rewrite each other

Trade a draft of a poem with another person. Each of you gets to rewrite the other's poem, then keep the results as his or her own.

email cutup

Start by having an email discussion/conversation/argument about some topic: your love lives, global warming, movies, technology, writing, death, racism. Write each other every day for a week. At the end of the week, print out your emails. Circle lines and phrases, together or separately, that seem charged with poetry. Get together and make a poem out of what you have.

word sculpture

In the last chapter, I suggested taking language off the page and making it three-dimensional. Do this with an artist who works with found materials, or who creates more traditional sculpture, or with another writer.

make a movie

With another writer, make two movies, each based on a poem by one of you. It could be as simple as recording each other while you recite. You could film a scene or event with the poem as voice-over: car trip, ocean waves, something happening on the street. Think about how your words might intersect/interact with moving images. Talk about your ideas, so the movies are truly a joint effort. If you like the results, post them on YouTube.

this interpretive dance will show you how i feel

Invite a dancer to perform with you at an open mic. The dancer may already have a project; you could create words/poems to interact with the movement. The idea of "dance" could branch out: someone doing yoga while you read, an interpreter signing your poems. How about a couple doing the tango as you read a poem about Argentina?

❋ 34

do-overs and revisions

If you don't think your work needs revision, here's a tip: Don't try to be a poet. You will never—I mean never—be any good.

If you take your art seriously, you will write the poem again and again until you get it right, or as close to right as you can make it. Revision separates the professionals from the amateurs and wannabes.

A lot of people get hung up on revision. How do you know if your work is any good? How can you be objective about your work, so you can figure out what it needs? How do you know what to let go of and what to keep? How do you know when a poem is finished? How do you keep from losing interest in the process that felt so great at first, but now feels like you're hacking through vines with a butter knife for a machete?

Welcome to the jungle.

Here is what I know about revision: It's not so much a process of editing as of making unexpected discoveries.

By that I mean that there are no answers to those questions about revision. There are only the decisions you make, and if you're lucky, they are the right ones for the work at hand. You can increase your luck by developing your skills. Instead of blind decisions, you'll make choices based on what you have learned about language.

If you are going it alone, you're relying on your best instincts, on what you are learning from reading poetry, and from reading books like this one (which is a very small starting point). If you're showing your work to a group, you are likely fielding several critiques, and possibly contradictory suggestions.

Still, there are guidelines. I'll list what mine are, currently, in the next section. Not all of them may be yours; as you continue to write, your aesthetic develops, and may well change. Lately I've been more interested in surprise than in story. My own guidelines have changed; I'll revise toward mystery more often. So use what follows if it's helpful, and realize that some poems will work out, but most won't.

What did I just say? *Most won't.* Work on them anyway. The published books that writers leave are a small part of the work they have done. Don't be discouraged if many of your poems fail. They are *supposed* to fail, to teach you that you have to keep going and try out new strategies.

the patient

Here's a common metaphor for a poem: A patient lies on a steel table, while everyone—practiced surgeons and amateurs—sharpens their instruments. Let's suppose your poem is on the table. How do you keep from killing it?

1. *Leave it alone.* This is a common prescription, and a good one. Once you've written it, put it away for at least several days. You will see problems and possibilities you could not see in the glow of inspiration; that is, you will see your poem a bit more as though someone else wrote it. The less you feel like you wrote it, the more you can see what it needs.
2. *Find the heat.* What feels essential—the thing without which the whole piece doesn't work? Can you distill that for yourself, or write a few words about it? It's very important to figure this out—not necessarily in the first or even third draft. But until you understand the core of your poem, you won't be able to finish it, because you won't know what you're trying to do. Why did you write this? Find the pulse of your poem, the core idea or lines, and rewrite toward that energy or driving idea. Sometimes the poem itself will tell you what you are saying. It might be different from what you thought you wanted to say. Think about theme, but let the language lead you.
3. *Diction.* Is your poem talky, lofty, comic, earnest, passionate, coolly observant? How convincing is the voice of the poem? Is there more than one voice? How are they interacting? Your diction, or word choice, has a lot to do with determining the tone. Try out different word choices—"walk" is usually more effective than "ambulate," "maybe" is more casual than "perhaps," one kind of person might "complain" while another would definitely "bitch." Choose the accurate, precise word. Sylvia Plath used *Roget's Thesaurus* so often she called herself "Roget's trollop."
4. *Detail.* Most people have difficulty writing with sufficient sensory detail. You may think you are being quite specific when you're not. Usually, you can go much further into an image than you think. Lean on your imagery until it gives up more than an adjective or two to describe something. See how microscopic you can be, and

then pull back as needed. In "From My Window," C. K. Williams describes watching one man pushing his friend in a wheelchair; as the wheelchair reaches the curb, the first man loses control, and they both fall:

> . . . and they both tumble, the one slowly, almost gracefully
> sliding in stages from his seat,
> his expression hardly marking it, the other staggering over him,
> spinning heavily down,

In fact, the entire fall takes four long lines to describe. How much richer and more vivid this is than "He loses control of the wheelchair, and they fall."

Sometimes you'll have plenty of detail, but it's pointless—that is, it doesn't lead toward the core of the poem. Often the detail is narrative: "We were roommates in the dorms at college and then she had this boyfriend who kept coming around with his six-packs of Bud Light, and he left the cans all over, and that was the same year my cousin got fired . . ." Meanwhile, the poem is supposed to lead to this friend's miscarriage. The writer got sidetracked. Revise toward significant detail.

5. *Rhythm, rhyme, sound.* A poem is a series of connections. You can't look at rhythms without looking at your line breaks, since they affect rhythm and pacing. A word with a different sound may change the tone of your piece, and the rhythm, too. The same with syntax: If you change your sentence structure, rhythm and meaning and tone can all shift. Get your ear down to the poem and listen; revise toward musicality.

   If you can't hear the music, mark stresses on the page. Triple-space your lines, and go slowly over each one, until you can hear that line aloud or in your head.
6. *Tension and surprise.* Develop oppositional elements: good and

evil, light and dark, joy and sorrow, the mundane and the extraordinary. If your poem is too pretty, it needs edge. If it's graphically violent, it may need some tenderness. Does your poem incorporate surprise—at the level of language (a word or image that leaps in an unexpected direction), and/or at the level of its structure? Does it surprise at the opening, in the middle, at the end? Is there so much surprise that the reader is left with nothing else? Is it so predictable that the poem has no movement from where it opened to where it ends?

7. *The intellectual and the intuitive.* Notice whether you have more head than heart in your poem. You want balance—not a huge head on a spindly body, or a big, bleeding heart with a tiny head attached. Think about what ideas underlie your poem. Suppose you've written a draft whose idea so far is this: "My friend doesn't want anything to do with me now, and I'm hurt and confused." If that's your topic, think deeply. How do we damage each other? How strong are the threads that connect us, and what happens when they are broken?

the laying on of hands

Take a poem that isn't working, or a handful of poems, and try these exercises.

1. *Change the tone or mood.* Take a serious poem and rewrite it as a humorous one, or vice versa. An earnest poem can be made ironic.
2. *Change the syntax and sentence lengths.* First, see how long or short your sentences are and how/whether their length varies. Try highlighting successive sentences in different colors, so you get a feel for your pacing. To diagram syntax, draw a line under the subjects of your sentences, a double line under the verbs, brackets around

clauses, and parentheses around phrases. Or use highlighting again. Study your habits, to identify your strengths and limitations.

3. *Get rid of your adjectives and adverbs.* Rewrite nouns and verbs to make them more vivid: "monolith" instead of "enormous mountain," "shuffled" instead of "walked slowly." Then, maybe, put a few adverbs and adjectives back in.
4. *Rewrite your poem by imitating another poet's style.* Here are some suggestions to start with. First, familiarize yourself with their work and figure out what seems characteristic of each writer. Use the guidelines from chapter 30, "A Poem You Love: Close Reading," as a starting point. Then recast one of your poems as if it were written by each of these contemporary poets:

    Jack Gilbert
    Lucille Clifton
    Sharon Olds
    John Ashbery
    Dean Young
    Wanda Coleman
    Li-Young Lee

5. *If your poem opens with an image, open with a statement instead.* Or vice versa. This may mean reorganizing your poem to begin with a different line, or writing a new line or two.
6. *Intensify the metaphorical level of your poem.* Locate your metaphors and extend them. Is there a place you can add a metaphor or simile and go further with what you are trying to say?
7. *Reduce a longer poem to ten lines.* Keep only what seems absolutely necessary.
8. *Extend a short poem (a page or less) to two pages.* If the lines are short, extend them as well. Add more physical detail, more emotional and intellectual information.

9. *Take every long sentence in your poem* (or every line, if you are not writing sentences) *and cut out words to make it shorter.*
10. *Take a narrative poem that covers a lot of territory, and cut it to talk about one moment in the poem.* Expand that moment until it's a poem of its own.
11. *Tell the story behind the metaphor* if your poem is basically metaphor—as in, "That was the winter of our love, / our words froze in our mouths."

You are likely to feel resistance to some of these exercises. Maybe you're happy with your line breaks and don't want to change them. Maybe you don't want to tell the story behind the winter of your love. The point of these exercises is simple: *Get the words and ideas in motion again.* The more you hold on to your writing, the less you will be able to discard moments that don't work and discover moments that do. Maybe you won't find a better line length, but in changing lines, you may discover some new language. Maybe your narrative poem will fracture into seven lovely lyrics. You can't know unless you are willing to reexamine what you've already written. And you can always go back to your earlier draft. The work you've done won't be wasted.

two draftings

The first step in revision—figuring out where the problems and opportunities of the poem lie—is often easier than the second step of solving those problems and building on the opportunities. The second step can take many drafts and much frustration; it involves trying different paths, many of which will be dead ends. But along with the dead ends, there are any number of elegant solutions that could make the poem work.

Keep in mind that *you can only revise to the level of your skills at this moment.*

Microsurgery

The harmonicas are tarnished where my lips
touched them, they have trembled with happiness
but also with pain, with bent notes
and lonely songs.

Those lines are from an early draft of my poem "Fever Blues." I knew I wanted talk about music as an expression of both happiness and difficulty, and I knew that so far, the language was boring. The problem here, after the description of the harmonicas as "tarnished," is a lack of sufficient detail. Or, I could simply say that the language is ordinary, pedestrian, and general. Also, there is the cliché, "lonely songs." I often do what I call "the comb-over"—taking those thin areas and adding in more texture, more detail, more energy of language. This moment was in need of a comb-over.

I don't remember the exact steps I took in revising this passage, but here are examples of the way I would have approached it.

First, I could have extended what I meant by "happiness" and "pain":

I have played them after losing love,
And after finding it again.

That's not much better. Although it has more detail, losing love and finding it are generic. Yawn. What if I were to try a metaphor or simile?

I have played them like . . . like . . . funeral instruments? Oboes? Something low, dirgelike? Harmonica, mouth organ, funeral march . . . nada, nada, nada.

Another dead end. What if I moved away from a simile for playing, and focused on the speaker?

> I have played them as though I were drowning,
> as though I'd been hauled up from some depths.

This direction seems more promising. But I'll try out more ideas. This time I'll change something else. What if instead of saying, "I have played them," I make the harmonicas do something?

> They have sung . . .

Okay, so they have sung. They have sung with happiness? I'm back to a statement as boring as the original.

Now, the next part is the part I can't teach; it's the leap. Here are the lines I finally ended up with:

> They have sung while handling the snakes of sorrow,
> happiness has knocked them down like a fit.

Where did these lines come from? Since I was writing about the blues and thinking about the South, I remembered that Southern churches once featured snake handlers—maybe they still do—and I recalled a scene I'd seen in a movie, people passing out in church when they were struck with the Holy Spirit. I used those abstractions of "pain" (which became "sorrow") and "happiness," but I located them inside a concrete metaphor: sorrows are like snakes we have to handle, and sometimes happiness just enters us and overtakes us. The metaphors fit the poem, intensifying the bluesy territory. Before getting to those lines I remember that I played with the music of the lines as well. Listen to the lines aloud, to the *s* sounds, to the second line's forceful KNOCKED them DOWN like a FIT.

This is how I work on individual moments in a poem.

Learn strategies, be stubborn, and wait—pray—for the leap.

Major surgery

Sometimes an entire poem is ill-conceived, or derivative, or simply doesn't measure up. Here are two of my poems. The first was published in a literary journal, but I never included it in a book. The second is from my collection *Tell Me.*

SEPTEMBER

At first
you barely notice
the bush of white flowers
on the dry hill
as you hike towards the glittering
weed-fringed pond,
but the sudden
vibrating blue wire
of a dragonfly
makes you stop on the path
to see that everything
is in motion: above
the blossoms a shirring chorus
of iridescent flies, fat
trembling bees, moths,
the small winged life
of the world darting
and dipping incessantly,
pale seed puffs
streaming on the air,
pollen burning
the back of your throat,
every heavy cell of your body
humming, preparing to rise.

ONSET

Watching that frenzy of insects above the bush of white flowers,
bush I see everywhere on hill after hill, all I can think of
is how terrifying spring is, in its tireless, mindless replications.
Everywhere emergence: seed-case, chrysalis, uterus, endless
manufacturing.
And the wrapped stacks of styrofoam cups in the grocery, lately
I can't stand them, the shelves of canned beans and soups, freezers
of identical dinners; then the snowflake-diamond-snowflake of the
rug
beneath my chair, rows of books turning their backs,
even my two feet, how they mirror each other oppresses me,
the way they fit so perfectly together, how I can nestle one big toe
into the other
like little continents that have drifted; my God the unity of
everything,
my hands and eyes, yours, doesn't that frighten you sometimes,
remembering
the pleasure of nakedness in fresh sheets, all the lovers there before
you,
beside you, crowding you out. And the scouring griefs,
don't look at them all or they'll kill you, you can barely encompass
your own;
I'm saying I know all about you, whoever you are, it's spring
and it's starting again, the longing that begins, and begins, and
begins.

I consider "Onset" to be a revision of "September," a poem I no longer like much. The radical difference in these two poems is perhaps an indication of how much needs to change for a true revisioning. "Onset" is truer to my original impulse, the one that got me writing about the insects and flowers in the first place—a sense of being appalled by all this sameness, rather than the transcendent moment recorded in "September," which in truth I never felt. So there's a fidelity to my sense of the world that I feel the second poem rendered more successfully.

Additionally, I'm bothered in "September" by how much the voice sounds like a poor imitation of Mary Oliver. Her work expresses her own sensibilities about the natural world; in "September" I felt I'd grafted on a certain inauthentic voice—maybe because all along I was detailing an inauthentic experience. "September" also ends with an uplifting moment that seems to me both easy and clichéd—here we are rising, hallelujah. I don't buy it for a minute.

I completed "Onset" about five years after writing "September." Maybe that, too, is an indication that the poem you need to write may take some time to mature underground.

8/3

The
North American
Review

The editors regret that the enclosed contribution is not adapted to the particular needs of the NAR at the present time. We are therefore returning it, with thanks for your courtesy in giving us an opportunity to examine it.

UNIVERSITY OF NORTHERN IOWA, CEDAR FALLS, IOWA 50614

Crazyhorse

Thank you for offering your work to *Crazyhorse*. We regret that it does not fit our current needs.

The Editors

Gettysburg
The Gettysburg Review

Thank you for letting us consider your manuscript. We regret that it does not suit our present needs.

The Fall of Saigon

Gettysburg College, Gettysburg, Penns

THE PARIS REVIEW
541 East 72nd Street
New York, NY 10021

Thank you for submitting your manuscript to The Paris Review. We regret that we are not able to make use of it at this time.

Yours sincerely,

The Editors

THE THREEPENNY REVIEW

P.O. Box 9131
Berkeley, California
94709

Kim—

Sorry, none quite right. I almost took "Stop" but it falters at the end, overcome by misguided niceness—it needs to have the courage of its own convictions.

Best,

W

⁂ 35

publishing & the pinocchio syndrome

So maybe you take your poems to your girlfriend, or your husband, or your friend, and they all love them. *You're so talented,* they tell you. They actually cry. They say, *I am going to keep these close to my heart.* But then you take those same poems to a creative writing class or a workshop, and those people say, *I don't understand; what is this about?* And *You have to get rid of all these clichés. This is so sentimental.* They poke and prod one of your poems until what had seemed to you a living, vibrant creature now seems like an abused animal. There's your poem, barely moving. Are they right? Are they idiots? You don't know. But you do what you can. You take suggestion A, and ignore suggestions B and C—everyone seems to have contradictory suggestions—and you work some more. You bring your poems back to the workshop, or to another writer friend, and at last you feel they are as ready as they are going to get.

Now you send your poems to the editors of several established literary journals that publish poetry. You even try *The New Yorker*. Sure, they probably get a lot of submissions, but your work is good. Your girlfriend *cried*. By the sixth or seventh draft, your workshop thought that one particularly troublesome opening had finally been smoothed out. Surely the *New Yorker* editors will recognize the power of your work.

After a very long wait—a few months to a year or more—your poems come back with form rejections.

> Dear ——, Thank you for submitting your work to ——. Unfortunately we cannot use it at this time.
>
> Sincerely,
>
> The Editors

In some cases, you simply never hear from the editors at all.

Either way, it's as though the poems have fallen into a black hole, all the love and energy you put in sucked right out of them.

Are the editors right? Are they idiots?

As you hacked through the jungle, you thought your butter knife had been honed to a pretty sharp blade. You thought you were making progress.

Now, all you have to show for your hard work, your dreams of literary fame and fortune, or at least recognition and a small check, your hopes for a book one day—all you have is *Sincerely, The Editors.*

This is the awful moment when you see that today, at least, you have failed. It feels terrible.

When my first poetry collection, *The Philosopher's Club*, was a finalist for the Barnard New Women Poets Prize—there were three finalists, and one would be selected to have her book published—I was ecstatic. In the weeks before the final decision I went around thinking, *Please please please please please pick me pick me pick me.* I tried to tell myself, *I probably won't win.* But there were only three of us, chosen from several hundred. The odds were good. I was thirty-four years old, two years out of graduate school, teaching several grueling composition classes at San Francisco State. I had published a few poems. I had been seriously writing and studying poetry for nearly seven years. I was ready.

When my manuscript wasn't selected, I took my usual run in Golden Gate Park. I cried as I ran, and the words in my head now were, *You'll never have a book. You'll never have a book. You aren't good enough.*

For the next several years, I submitted my manuscript, every year, to every first-book competition in the United States (that was, and is, how most first books of poetry are published by small presses and university presses). I racked up a lot of fees for copying and submitting, and a lot of letters informing me that So-and-So had won the competition. Thank you for submitting your work. *Sincerely, The Editors.*

You think you're ready. But most of the time, you are wrong. This is what the rejection slips are telling you. They are telling you that a lot of people out there are working very hard and writing very well. Possibly they have been at it longer. Possibly they are more talented.

By the time *The Philosopher's Club* was published, I was forty. I had revised or outright jettisoned nearly half of the poems that had been part of the book when it was a finalist for the Barnard prize. In the years it took to publish *The Philosopher's Club*, I wrote a better book, one I can go back to now and feel okay about, instead of wanting to track down all the copies in existence and burn them.

This is not to say, *Persist and you will overcome all obstacles.* But be patient. Adrienne Rich once wrote a book titled *A Wild Patience Has Taken Me This Far.* Wild patience is what you need. Publishing is competitive. Editors of journals receive thousands of submissions—many of them, truthfully, pretty bad, written by people who have not bothered to learn their craft before sending in their late-night inspirations. In addition, there are many competent poems that don't go far enough into wildness or surprise or complication or whatever else a particular editor is hoping to find. And there are a few marvelously realized pieces an editor will respond to immediately—or possibly miss, due to illness or a hangover or several other human reasons. Somewhere in this mix are your own poems.

Of course editors are selecting according to their own taste. Of course, in the case of a university journal, graduate students, and not longtime editors, may be reading your work. You can't always know. Maybe your work *is* ready. But assume that it isn't, quite. You don't get out of the jungle easily. You'll need to sharpen your blade even more.

Once, when I was whining to a friend on the phone about a rejection—everyone gets rejections, even writers who have published several books, even Pulitzer Prize winners—she interrupted me and said, "Oh, Kim, butch it up."

This is good advice for a sensitive poet.

i'm only a wooden writer

The logic of publishing is this:

Just because a poem is rejected doesn't mean it's bad.

Just because a poem is published doesn't mean it's any good.

And: The work is more important than the publication, but you may not really understand this until you are published.

Also, it is actually easy to get published. Somewhere. By someone. The problem is that this won't be enough. You will want to be published somewhere else, somewhere better. Your first publication was in a stapled local zine, and now you want to see your work in an established literary journal. If you attain that, you will wonder why you didn't win the yearly prize given to poems published in the journal. Next you will want your own book, and then you will feel a pressing need to achieve a second book, to prove to yourself that the first wasn't a fluke. You will want awards for your books, then big grants and fellowships and endowed chairs, and after all of this, you will really want eternal youth.

But if you are not yet published, nothing I have just said will mean anything to you. It's natural to want to share your work in print, to have it judged worthy by an editor, but don't fall prey to what I call the Pinocchio Syndrome: Publish me! I'm only a wooden writer! Make me a real writer!

The work is more important.

Let this mantra save you, when you start collecting rejections.

some tips on submission

The basics of submitting your work were covered in my previous book, *The Poet's Companion*. That was written when most poems were submitted by snail mail; now more and more journals are asking for electronic submissions, and online journals have proliferated. Most print journals also have an online presence. Here's a brief recap of how to submit your work, and how to make the process work for you:

- *Read the guidelines and follow them.* You can find sites with links to literary journals in the back of this book, under "Poems and Poetry Resources Online." The journals have posted their guidelines. Don't send ten pages if the editors specify five. Usually, four to six pages of poetry is plenty. Many journals have reading periods; you'll want to know this so you don't submit during a time when your poems will sit unread, or simply be returned to you. In the case of print journals, submission information is usually in the small print in the front of the journal, or posted on the journal's web site.
- *Be professional.* No typos, no spelling errors, no calligraphy or clever fonts. Put your name, address, phone, and email on every page.
- *Write a brief cover letter.* Don't explain your poems; just ask the editors to consider your poems, mention any publications and your school, if you're in a writing program. Include a self-addressed stamped envelope if you are submitting by snail mail.

- *Submit simultaneously.* I suggest sending to journals that accept simultaneous submissions. If they don't accept simultaneous submissions, you may opt to do so anyway, but you'll have to pull a poem if it is accepted by two journals, and risk annoying an editor.
- *Revise.* Don't send out anything you have just written, no matter how brilliant it may seem to you. Wait. Get critiques, if you can, from other writers. A first or second or third draft isn't yet a finished poem.
- *Focus.* The number of places to send your work is overwhelming. Where do you start? Visit the poetry sites listed in the back of this book to find literary journals. Maybe you are familiar with some already, or your school publishes a magazine. Ask friends, teachers, and other writers to suggest journals you might want to read and/or send your work to. You can also buy *Poet's Market* (www.poetsmarket .com), which contains a wealth of information about submitting your work, as well as useful articles.
- *Work your way up. Poet's Market* has a handy system of Roman numerals identifying which places are open to new writers, and which are more competitive. Start by submitting your work to those journals that are ranked I or II. Of course you don't *want* to do this. You want to send your work to *The New Yorker*, a IV, or to *Poetry* (also a IV), or to some other well-regarded journal that receives huge numbers of submissions. The problem with this approach is that you will get discouraged quickly as the form rejections pile up. If, on the other hand, you submit your work to a local zine, or a beginner-friendly Internet site, you will likely bask in the glow of your success, and be encouraged to continue working.
- *Network.* Every human endeavor, including the publishing of poetry, is rife with politics. If your work is that of a beginner, it doesn't matter what well-known poet you show it to. But if you're seriously writing and studying, it's helpful to talk to other poets about publishing, and to work with an established writer at a college or university, or at a writers' conference. This doesn't mean thrusting your sheaf of poems

at said established writer. But many writers are happy, when they see good work, to help an emerging poet.

A caveat here: A number of people I have met at writers' conferences know all about publishing, and not nearly enough about how to write. If you attend a conference or M.F.A. program expecting insider secrets, or hoping that some well-known writer will "discover" you and become your mentor, you may be disappointed. Plan to connect with other poets, to study your craft, and by all means, to learn how the literary world works.

- *Balance.* The greater proportion of your time should be spent reading and writing. The time it takes to submit work is time taken away from improving your skills. When you become a better writer, publication will be easier. Try not to obsess over publication; obsess over getting "the best words in the best order," as Samuel Taylor Coleridge said. That's what will turn you from a wooden writer into a real one.

36

mirror at the end of the road

In my end is my beginning.

—*T. S. Eliot*

What is your definition of success as a writer?

I was once asked by a man who had come to me for a consultation, "How long should I give this thing before I know if I'm any good?" I couldn't give him a definitive answer. I suggested that seven to ten years was a reasonable apprenticeship, but something might happen sooner—or later. You can't set up a business plan for art. You have to go forth blindly, armed with your passion, and try to learn the skills you need to make good poems. You have to fail, often, and be willing to go on.

I have seen a number of writers with talent—the kind of raw talent that can be recognized even in beginners—who didn't have the desire, or the wild patience, to pursue writing. I've seen people whose initial work was unpromising (I was certainly one of them) and who, through sheer, dogged persistence, eventually made poems I would not have thought them capable of.

Maybe your definition of success is that you will continue to write and learn. As a musician, that's what I want with my harmonica playing—to keep music close to me, and to make my own version of it. Music is an art I want to master to the best of my ability, so I will keep practicing.

When I took trapeze, success meant simply climbing the ladder every time, doing something I was afraid to do. I even took a few swings, finally, without the aid of ropes and harness. Soon afterward I decided that I wanted to spend my time on other pursuits. But I loved the time I had spent flying.

Maybe you are the kind of person who likes to sample new things, to gain some understanding, and then try other adventures. Maybe you want to delve more deeply into writing, and share it with a few close friends and family members. You are the only one who knows what it means to "succeed" at writing. If you think that outward success as a writer will solve your loneliness, or bolster your self-worth, or radically change you, you are likely to be disappointed, rather than gratified, by the external success that does come your way.

If you want to be a professional poet and publish books, understand that there isn't much money to be made. You will still need another source of income: restaurant work, corporate work, teaching, selling insurance or cars. You will have to make time for your creative work, time that will be taken away from other pursuits: time with family and friends, cooking or gardening or social activism.

And if you find you'd rather do something else, that you have other gifts and passions, poetry will still sustain you as a reader.

It may be time to stop reading this book, and turn to some great poetry. There are so many astonishing writers this book has failed even to mention. I hope you will go on to discover some of them, the great power and humanity of their work.

It may be time to reread the journal you've been keeping, to see what has happened in your life and your imagination, and what can be made of it.

In "Tear It Down," Jack Gilbert writes, "We should insist while there is still time." We must, he says, "wade mouth-deep into love." If writing poetry is truly your love, don't waste another minute. Insist. Look for the next step in your creative journey, and don't worry about where or how that journey will end. Let your genius guide you.

Breathe in, and begin.

Sometimes I go about weeping, and all the while I am being carried across the sky on a great wind.

—*Chippewa song*

appendix A

poems & poetry resources online

About.com: Poetry (http://poetry.about.com)
Articles, biographies of classic poets, interviews with contemporary poets, contests and awards, links to poets online.

Academy of American Poets (http://www.poets.org)
An extensive site with poems, essays, audio recordings, and publishing FAQs.

Association of Writers and Writing Programs (http://www.awpwriter.org)
AWP is an organization which supports writers and academic creative writing programs. Information on M.F.A. programs, writers' conferences, jobs for writers.

Bartleby.com (http://www.bartleby.com)
"The preeminent Internet publisher of literature, reference, and verse." Look for the classic poets here, as well as poetry by category: War Poetry, Irish Verse. You

can also find a dictionary, a thesaurus, quotations, the King James Bible, Strunk and White's *Elements of Style*, and much more.

Favorite Poem Project (http://www.favoritepoem.org)
The results of former United States Poet Laureate Robert Pinksy's project, asking Americans to read and talk about their favorite poems. See the podcasts here (there's also a book and DVD).

Gotham Writers' Workshop (http://www.writingclasses.com)
Online workshops for all kinds of writing, including poetry, offered by faculty who are established writers. Authorized provider of Continuing Education Units.

Indiefeed: Performance Poetry (http://www.indiefeedpp.libsyn.com)
Podcasts of spoken word and slam artists.

Library of Congress (Poetry Home) (http://www.loc.gov/poetry)
You can find the current Poet Laureate of the United States here, along with poetry news and links. The "Poet Vision" series and the "Poet and the Poem" series feature webcasts of several well-known poets discussing their craft.

New Letters on the Air (http://www.newletters.org/ontheair.asp)
Interviews with writers, and weekly podcasts.

Poetry Daily (http://www.poems.com), Verse Daily (http://www.versedaily.org)
Each of these sites posts a poem a day by established and emerging writers. Poetry Daily offers links to prose features on poetry, as well as poetry news and reviews. Verse Daily offers monthly poetry-related features.

Poetry Foundation (http://www.poetryfoundation.org)
An extensive site featuring *Poetry* magazine, poets, poems, podcasts, blogs, reading guides, and more.

Poetry Slam, Inc. (http://www.poetryslam.com)
Information on tournaments, slam poets, forums and discussions.

Poetry Society of America (http://www.psa.org)

PSA promotes poetry in America through various initiatives including Poetry in Motion, which places placards of poems on buses and subways. Events, awards, and resources including poetry journals; contests; colonies, conferences, and festivals; and poetry for children.

Poets and Writers (http://www.pw.org)

The online presence of what is essentially the "trade magazine" for writers. Listings of grants and awards available to writers, literary magazines, small presses, literary events calendars, articles on writing, nationwide directory of poets and writers.

Shaw Guides: Writers' Conferences and Workshops (http://writing.shawguides.com)

A national and international directory.

UCLA Extension (http://www.uclaextension.edu)

Offers online poetry and writing workshops with established authors.

Web del Sol (http://www.webdelsol.com)

Blogs, RSS feeds, "Top 50 Literary Journals," writing, Lit and Talk Radio, reviews, and much more.

appendix B

recommended reading

Addonizio, Kim, and Dorianne Laux. *The Poet's Companion: A Guide to the Pleasures of Writing Poetry*. W. W. Norton & Company, 1997.

Writing exercises and essays on the poet's craft and process, from line breaks to writer's block to publishing.

Boland, Eavan, and Mark Strand, eds. *The Making of a Poem: A Norton Anthology of Poetic Forms.* W. W. Norton & Company, 2001.

Introductions to various forms, along with their history and several chronological examples.

Boland, Eavan, and Edward Hirsch, eds. *The Making of a Sonnet: A Norton Anthology*. W. W. Norton & Company, 2008.

Over three hundred sonnets, with essays discussing the form in each century;

includes variations on the sonnet as well as a collection of sonnets from other countries.

Costanzo, Gerald, and Jim Daniels, eds. *American Poetry: The Next Generation.* Carnegie-Mellon University Press, 2000.
Poets born since 1960, with a selection of poems from each.

Chang, Victoria, ed. *Asian American Poetry: The Next Generation.* University of Illinois Press, 2004.
Emerging poets under forty.

Dobyns, Stephen. *Best Words, Best Order.* 2nd edition. Palgrave Macmillan, 2003.
Challenging, insightful essays on the craft. The concluding chapters examine four writers: Rainer Maria Rilke, Osip Mandelstam, Anton Chekhov, and Yannis Ritsos.

Ferguson, Margaret, Mary Jo Salter, and Jon Stallworthy, eds. *The Norton Anthology of Poetry.* 5th edition. W. W. Norton & Company, 2005.
The English canon, from *Beowulf* to writers born in the mid-twentieth century.

Fussell, Paul. *Poetic Meter & Poetic Form.* 1st edition. McGraw-Hill Humanities/Social Sciences/Languages, 1979.
A brilliant, now-classic book on the workings of meter and traditional forms.

Glazner, Gary Mex, ed. *Poetry Slam: The Competitive Art of Performance Poetry.* Manic D Press, 2000.
The slam scene, including history, poems from slam champions, and competition rules.

Graham, David and Kate Sontag, eds. *After Confession: Poetry as Autobiography.* Graywolf Press, 2001.
Essays from various contemporary poets about the first-person lyric and the limits and opportunities of the "confessional mode."

Hamill, Sam, ed. *Crossing the Yellow River: Three Hundred Poems from the Chinese.* BOA Editions, 2000.

Classic Chinese poets, from 330 B.C. to the sixteenth century.

Harper, Michael, and Anthony Walton, eds. *The Vintage Book of African American Poetry.* Vintage Books, 2000.

From slave-born poets to contemporary writers, with biographical notes and commentary.

Henderson, Bill, ed. *The Pushcart Prize Anthology.* Pushcart Press.

A yearly anthology of "the best from the small presses." Poetry, fiction, and essays are nominated by editors-at-large and literary magazine editors, and then selected by each year's guest editors.

Hirsch, Edward. *How to Read a Poem and Fall in Love with Poetry.* Harvest Books, 2000.

A practicing poet who loves poetry introduces readers to his insights and enthusiasms.

Hoagland, Tony. *Real Sofistikashun: Essays on Poetry and Craft.* Graywolf Press, 2006.

Essays on contemporary poets and poetic strategies.

Hyde, Lewis. *The Gift: Creativity and the Artist in the Modern World.* Vintage, 2007.

A reissue of the classic, thought-provoking book first published twenty-five years ago with the subtitle *Imagination and the Erotic Life of Poetry.*

Joris, Pierre, and Jerome Rothenberg, eds. *Poems for the Millennium: The University of California Book of Modern and Postmodern Poetry.* University of California Press, vol. 1, 1995; vol. 2, 1998.

A wide-ranging, unique anthology of modern and postmodern poetry, in two volumes, that "tests the limits of poetry," organized in "galleries."

Kowit, Steve. *In the Palm of Your Hand: The Poet's Portable Workshop.* Tilbury House, 1995.
A clear and accessible introduction to writing poems, with step-by-step writing exercises and advice.

Lehman, David, series ed. *The Best American Poetry.* Scribner.
A yearly anthology, the selections chosen each year by a well-established poet.

Lehman, David, ed. *The Best American Erotic Poems from 1800 to the Present.* Scribner, 2008.
From Francis Scott Key and Edgar Allan Poe to contemporary writers.

Levin, Phillis, ed. *The Penguin Book of the Sonnet: 500 Years of a Classic Tradition in English.* Penguin, 2001.
Over six hundred sonnets, including many by twentieth-century authors.

Marshall, Tod, ed. *Range of the Possible: Conversations with Contemporary Poets.* Eastern Washington University Press, 2002.
Interviews with poets including several of their poems and their commentary.

McClatchy, J. D., ed. *The Vintage Book of Contemporary World Poetry.* Vintage Books, 1996.
A strong selection of poets from around the globe.

Pinsky, Robert. *The Sounds of Poetry: A Brief Guide.* Farrar, Straus & Giroux, 1998.
Close readings and analysis by the former United States Poet Laureate.

Rilke, Rainer Maria. *Letters to a Young Poet.* Trans. M. D. Herter Norton. W. W. Norton & Company, 1993.
Rilke's letters were written to an aspiring poet. A classic and inspiring book on writing and the poetic spirit.

Theune, Michael, ed. *Structure and Surprise: Engaging Poetic Turns.* Teachers & Writers Collaborative, 2007.

A useful engagement with the architecture of poems. In each chapter, a different poet discusses a structure—meditative, ironic, confessional, elegiac—with several examples.

Turco, Lewis. *The Book of Forms: A Handbook of Poetics.* University Press of New England, 2000.
Everything you wanted to know about meter and form—a comprehensive reference.

Young, Kevin, ed. *Blues Poems.* Everyman's Library Pocket Series, Alfred A. Knopf, 2003.
Pre-World War II blues from Langston Hughes and others, several song lyrics, and modern and contemporary poems in the blues form or with a blues sensibility.

credits

Kim Addonizio: "What Do Women Want?" and "Onset" from *Tell Me: Poems* by Kim Addonizio. Copyright © 2000 by Kim Addonizio. Reprinted with the permission of BOA Editions, Ltd. www.boaeditions.org.

Doug Anderson: "A Bar in Argos" from *The Moon Reflected Fire*. Copyright © 1994 by Doug Anderson. Reprinted with the permission of Alice James Books.

George Bilgere: "The Good Kiss" from *The Good Kiss*, The University of Akron Press, copyright © 2001 by George Bilgere. Reprinted by permission of The University of Akron Press.

Robert Bly: "The Holy Longing" by Goethe, translated by Robert Bly, from *News of the Universe*, ed. by Robert Bly (Sierra Club Books, 1980). Reprinted by permission of Robert Bly.

Susan Browne: "Two Clerics Hacked to Death in Holy City" is reprinted by permission of the author. Copyright © 2008 by Susan Browne.

Lucille Clifton: "wishes for sons" from *Blessing the Boats: New and Selected Poems 1988–2000*. Copyright © 1991 by Lucille Clifton. Reprinted with the permission of BOA Editions, Ltd. www.boaeditions.org.

Billy Collins: "No Time" from *Nine Horses* by Billy Collins, copyright © 2002 by Billy Collins. Used by permission of Random House, Inc.

E. E. Cummings: Lines from "spoke joe to jack" copyright © 1940, 1968, 1991 by the Trustees for the E. E. Cummings Trust, from *Complete Poems: 1904–1962* by E. E. Cummings, ed. by George J. Firmage. Used by permission of Liveright Publishing Corporation.

Stephen Dobyns: "Desire" from *Body Traffic* by Stephen Dobyns, copyright © 1990 by Stephen Dobyns. Used by permission of Viking Penguin, a division of Penguin Group (USA) Inc.

Denise Duhamel: The selection from Denise Duhamel's *Mille et un sentiments* (Firewheel Editions, 2005) is reprinted here by permission of the author and Firewheel Editions.

Robert Duncan: From *The Opening of the Field*, copyright © 1960 by Robert Duncan. Reprinted by permission of New Directions Publishing Corp.

Russell Edson: "Baby Pianos" from *The Tormented Mirror* by Russell Edson, copyright © 2001. Reprinted by permission of The University of Pittsburgh Press.

Nick Flynn: "Bag of Mice" copyright © 2000 by Nick Flynn is reprinted from *Some Ether* with the permission of Graywolf Press, Saint Paul, Minnesota.

Louise Glück: "Gretel in Darkness" from *The First Four Books of Poems* by Louise Glück. Copyright © 1968, 1971, 1972, 1973, 1974, 1975, 1976, 1977, 1978, 1979, 1980, 1985, 1995 by Louise Glück. Reprinted by permission of HarperCollins Publishers. *Firstborn, Descending Figure, House on Marshland, Triumph of Achilles* (Ecco Press).

Tony Hoagland: From "Here in Berkeley," copyright © 1998 by Tony Hoagland, is reprinted from *Donkey Gospel*, and an excerpt from "Negative Capability" is reprinted from *Real Sofistikashun*, copyright © 2006 by Tony Hoagland, with the permission of Graywolf Press, Saint Paul, Minnesota.

Randall Jarrell: "The Death of the Ball Turret Gunner" from *The Complete Poems* by Randall Jarrell. Copyright © 1969, renewed by Mary von S. Jarrell. Reprinted by permission of Farrar, Straus and Giroux, LLC.

Denis Johnson: "Sway" from *The Incognito Lounge* by Denis Johnson, copyright © 1974, 1976, 1977, 1978, 1979, 1980, 1981, 1982 by Denis Johnson. Used by permission of Random House, Inc.

A. Van Jordan: "af.ter.glow" from *M-A-C-N-O-L-I-A: Poems* by A. Van Jordan. Copyright © 2004 by A. Van Jordan. Used by permission of W. W. Norton & Company, Inc.

Li-Young Lee: "Evening Hieroglyph" from *Behind My Eyes* by Li-Young Lee. Copyright © 2008 by Li-Young Lee. Used by permission of W. W. Norton & Company, Inc.

Gary Copeland Lilley: "Our Lady of the Birds" from *The Subsequent Blues.* Copyright © 2004 by Gary Copeland Lilley. Reprinted with the permission of Four Way Books, www.fourwaybooks.com

Charles Martin: From *The Poems of Catullus* tr. by Charles Martin, pp. 72, 85. Copyright © 1989 The John Hopkins University Press. Reprinted with permission of The Johns Hopkins University Press.

William Matthews: "Poem Ending with a Line from Dante" is reprinted by permission of Estate of William Matthews.

Marilyn Nelson: "Balance" is reprinted from *The Fields of Praise* by permission of Louisiana State University Press.

Sharon Olds: "Self-Portrait, Rear View" from *One Secret Thing* by Sharon Olds, copyright © 2008 by Sharon Olds. Used by permission of Alfred A. Knopf, a division of Random House, Inc.

Nancy K. Pearson: Section 1 and 2 of "Motel by the Hour" first published in *The Iowa Review* is reprinted by permission of the author. Copyright © 2008 by Nancy K. Pearson.

Lucia Perillo: From *The Body Mutinies* by Lucia Perillo. Copyright © 1996 Purdue University Press. Reprinted with permission. Unauthorized duplication not permitted.

Barbara Ras: From "Where I Go When I'm Out of My Mind" from *One Hidden Stuff* by Barbara Ras, copyright © 2006 by Barbara Ras. Used by permission of Penguin, a division of Penguin Group (USA) Inc.

Kay Ryan: "Blandeur" from *Say Uncle* is used by permission of Grove/Atlantic, Inc. Copyright © 2000 by Kay Ryan.

Clay Stockton: "The Pick-Up Artist in Spring" is reprinted by permission of the author. Copyright © Clay Stockton. This poem previously appeared at 14 by 14 (http://www.14by14.com).

Jean Toomer. From "Blood-Burning Moon" from *Cane* by Jean Toomer. Copyright 1923 by Boni & Liveright, renewed 1951 by Jean Toomer. Used by permission of Liveright Publishing Corporation.

Ellen Bryant Voigt: From "Variations: Two Trees," copyright © 1992, 2007 by Ellen Bryant Voigt from *Messenger: New and Selected Poems 1976–2006* by Ellen Bryant Voigt. Used by permission of W. W. Norton & Company, Inc.

Charles Harper Webb: "Prayer to Tear the Sperm-Dam Down" from *Amplified Dog* (Red Hen Press, 2006) is reprinted by permission of the publisher.

Elizabeth Winston: Photograph titled "Boats in Provincetown" is reprinted by permission. Copyright © by Elizabeth Winston.

C. D. Wright: Excerpt from "Nothing to Declare" from *Further Adventures with You.* Copyright © 1986 by C. D. Wright. Reprinted with the permission of Carnegie Mellon University Press, www.cmu.edu/universitypress.

Gary Young: From *Pleasure* (Heyday Books, 2006). Reprinted by permission of the publisher.

Ron Zak: Photographed titled "Hazel" from the series "American Pairs, Portraits, Aliases," 1975–1979. Used by permission of Ron Zak. Copyright © by Zakworld.com.

about the author

Kim Addonizio is the author of five books of poetry, including *Tell Me*, which was a National Book Award finalist. Her new collection, forthcoming from W. W. Norton, is *Lucifer at the Starlite*. Addonizio's work has received numerous honors, including two NEA Fellowships, a Guggenheim Fellowship, and a Pushcart Prize. Her other books include the novels *Little Beauties* and *My Dreams Out in the Street*. She teaches private writing workshops in Oakland, California, and online. Visit her web site at www.kimaddonizio.com.